ACHIEVE YOUR GOALS
AND FULFILL YOUR DREAMS
IN 31 DAYS

# *PROMISES*

## MARK C. OVERTON

**Promises:**
**Achieve Your Goals and Fulfill Your Dreams in 31 Days**

Copyright © 2024 by Mark C. Overton

ISBN: 978-1962497374(sc)

ISBN: 978-1962497381(e)

The Reading Glass Books
(888) 420-3050
www.readingglassbooks.com
production@readingglassbooks.com

The *Logos Bible* and *Merriam-Webster's Learner's Dictionary* tell us the meaning of a promise and its synonyms, respectively. As you read through each promise, ponder, *show*, and meditate on each Bible verse. Claim them over your life and go and do likewise; apply, put into practice, and live them out to receive his blessings. They're real! You'll discover God will do what He's promised. You have His word!

PROMISE

■noun

1 an assurance that one will do something or that something will happen.

▶ an indication that something is likely to occur: the promise of spring.

2 potential excellence.

■ verb

1 make a promise.

▶ (be promised) archaic be pledged to marry.

2 give good grounds for expecting.

3 (promise oneself) firmly intend.

—derivatives promiser noun

—origin Middle English: from Latin promissum 'something promised', neuter past participle of promittere 'put forth, promise' (from pro- 'forward' + mittere 'send').

**Commit**

To promise to do something.

**Swear**

To make a sincere statement that you are telling the truth.

**Guarantee**

To promise that something will happen.

**Vow**

To promise that you will do something (formal).

Undertake

To promise to do something (formal).

**Pledge**

To promise seriously and publicly to do something (mainly journalism).

**Vouchsafe**

To give, promise, or offer something to someone who you trust (formal).

**Give (someone) your word**

To promise to do something.

# CONTENTS

# *FOREWORD*

I love singing Russell Kelso Carter's hymn, *Standing on the Promises*: "Standing on the promises of Christ my King, Through eternal ages let his praises ring; Glory in the highest, I'll shout and sing, Standing on the promises of God." Great song, but what does it mean – this standing on the promises? How do you stand on His promises? What does the word promise mean to you? A promise is a vow, a commitment, a guarantee. Or so the book definition is, but when I say promise, what do you think of? Do you think of the crooked car salesman who told you there was nothing wrong with the car, and it was the cheapest one they had? Or maybe the politician who promises he won't raise taxes and he's on your side. Or perhaps it hits even closer to home. She promised to take you for better, worse, or richer or poorer. And when poorer and worse came, her promise was left with her. Stand on a promise – I don't think so; the last promise I stood on was broken.

A couple of years ago, we had a bad ice storm on a Friday night. One of our pastors arrived at the church Saturday morning to get ready for our Saturday night ser*vice* for young adults. The storm covered the parking lot with ice. Some other people were already there breaking up the ice so folk could get to church. The volunteers went in and got coffee to warm up, and he stayed outside and started working. He was glad they went inside because it wasn't long before he lost his balance. Both feet and the shovel went in the air, and the pastor landed on the hard ice. He saw nothing but sky overhead. Thankfully, no one was around. But now he'd to get up – without falling again. The pastor had

1

no such luck. He dropped one more time and saw nothing but the sky. Thankfully, no one was around. He got up this time using the shovel. Now, my colleague had another problem; the pain was unbearable. Lots of pain, and he was cold. And to go inside was defeat. After all, the helpers had worked for a long time without stopping. The Young Adults Pastor had been out there 15 minutes, and now he was going in. But it hurt so badly. He was so cold and carefully made his way inside. My coworker found the guys but couldn't tell them why he'd come inside for ego's sake. He could barely sip his coffee, and his rear end was hurting so badly. My associate wasn't about to tell them why he was inside. All pain and embarrassment because he couldn't trust what he was standing on. The ice was hard to walk on and painful when he fell. In life, broken promises are hard to stand on too; they're even more painful when what you were standing on-- a rock-solid foundation gives way.

Something to stand on that won't give way in tough times and for followers of Jesus Christ; we stand on the promises of God. You can find His promises in His Word – the Bible. It's our rock-solid foundation. The Bible is more than a book of stories about what happened 2,000 years ago. From its promises, we draw strength, find hope, and most of all, learn about the God who loves us. His word is powerful. His promises are real. It's the rock-solid foundation upon which we build our faith. You can stand on His promises you'll find in His Word.

In the end, the word promise means different things to different people. Mark, who joined First NLR in 2015, has structured this book's 31-day roadmap of God's promises around three guideposts: the promise's meaning, an engaging story of fulfillment, and fruitful application. The stories are inspiring. But more than the information, motivation, and practical guidance, what stands out is the appeal and journey to trust in and live out God's promises. You can receive 31 days of His blessings and favor every day and each month of the year. *Like* the story of Ezekiel in the Old Testament (Ezekiel 2:9 – 3:9), Mark had an encounter with His promises. No, Mark didn't eat a scroll with God's words. But they're a part of his life like the food he eats becomes part of him. He's an active member of our greeting ministry and supports outreach and Mission initiatives.

The Bible is also God's story of bringing salvation to us. He loves you and me so much. He gave us life and created us for our relationship with Him. When we sinned and broke that relationship, He gave us Jesus, his Son, to restore our relationship with Him. After He gave us the Holy Spirit, so we won't be alone. He then gave us the Bible. The Bible explains this and tells us this story. The Bible is our guidebook for living and can transform your life. His Word is to be the light guiding you in a dark world. His Word is to be your comfort in a storm. It's what you stand on. When you need a promise to stand on that won't fade away, you go to the Bible. It's filled with encouragement, blessing, guidance, and direction. It's our guidebook for living. Like Ezekiel eating the Word, you and I must do the same thing. Take His Word, break it down, and absorb it. Eat his words and grow. Fill your life with the Bible. God gave us His Word. Respond to His gift and realize you need more of the Bible.

Let me give you a couple of ways you can fill your life with Scripture:

1) Create and follow a plan to read the Bible. Spend time reading a *part* of the Bible until you think you understand it and can apply it to your life. Then move on.

2) Memorize Bible verses. Memorizing the Bible gives you a foundation to stand on when life overwhelms you. So, I've got a question: What promise are you standing on? What are your own best guesses? Somebody else's promises? The reason you keep falling and the reason you've so much pain is because you're standing on the wrong thing. Stand on God's promises. Read His promises and memorize them. Then, here's one more way to get more of the Bible in your life.

3) Join a Sunday school class. Also, to meet great people, Sunday school is one of the best places to learn more about God and faith. His promises succeed. But sometimes you need all the help you can get standing. Sunday school is that place. It's why you and I need

more of the Bible. When life's hard, I can stand on His rock-solid promises. What you stand on decides if you'll make it when life becomes difficult. These are His promises from His Word -- *Promise*. And as you hear or read His gift to you, eat His words – *achieve your goals and fulfill your dreams in 31 Days.*

Rod Loy

Lead Pastor, First Assembly North Little Rock

# INTRODUCTION

*Unveiling the Path of Abundance: Embracing God's Promises and Reaping His Blessings*

Mark C. Overton
November 27, 2023

Greetings, Riley.

I hope this message finds you well. Do you remember the childhood tradition of making a pinky promise to solidify our unbreakable bond as best friends? The simple gesture serves as a reminder of the value of keeping one's word – like Scout's honor! I want to share a story that embodies this principle. A couple had always been frugal with their money, and before he passed away, the husband made a solemn request for his wife to bury him with the $50,000 he had saved. She reluctantly agreed. However, she discreetly placed a small wooden box at the funeral into the casket. A friend asked if she had fulfilled her promise, to which she replied with confidence in her Christian beliefs, "Yes, I did. But I wrote a check." This anecdote beautifully illustrates the significance of honoring one's promises, even when faced with difficult decisions.

Similarly, failing to honor commitments can have significant consequences. Just imagine the impact on your reputation when you consistently disappoint clients and break promises. It's not uncommon to come across enticing offers that seem too good to be true, like the promise of a fortune through an advance fee scam. These schemes often involve a wealthy foreigner seeking help, transferring millions of dollars from their home country, and offering a sizable percentage as a reward for assistance. The pitch usually includes references to multi-million dollar sums and guarantees that you will receive a substantial portion for helping these "disadvantaged" individuals. The scam works by preying on your desire for quick wealth or alluring you with something too valuable to pass up. Have you been caught in this trap before? Have fraudsters deceived, cheated, or tricked you with promises of an easy fortune?

These experiences are reminders of the potential consequences that can come with breaking promises. Promises can cover various topics, from financial matters to personal commitments like quitting smoking or losing weight. In desperate situations, we may plead for divine intervention and make promises, saying things like, "If you help me out, I promise to serve you." We may also express our promises through actions, such as making military oaths or exchanging promise rings with our partners (from the "I Promise" to "I Do"). These acts signify our dedication and loyalty. For example, during a wedding rehearsal, the groom joked with the minister and asked him to leave out the traditional vows in exchange for $100. However, during the ceremony, when the minister asked him if he promised to bow down to his wife and fulfill her every desire, he hesitantly replied with a weak "I do." This humorous story illustrates how significant promises can be within the context of marriage.

In addition to personal relationships, commitments are apparent in various aspects of life. These include enduring friendships, the allegiance of college alumni to their alma mater, veterans' devotion to their country, and the loyalty citizens hold towards their nation. However, we must acknowledge that pledges without follow-through can result in unfulfilled promises. For instance, Social Security benefits pledged but only acted upon could become attainable if addressed promptly. This realization has raised concerns among 71 percent of Americans who fear Social Security may exhaust its funds during their lifetimes. The Veterans Administration also aims to fulfill President Lincoln's promise of caring for military personnel and their loved ones. Promises made by public figures like presidents carry significant weight as well. Some notable examples include President Reagan's refusal to engage in hostage trades, President H.W. Bush's famous "Read my lips; no new taxes," and President Obama's commitment to reject contributions from lobbyists and political action committees. Along with these promises, we are familiar with powerful speeches such as Martin Luther King Jr.'s "I Have a Dream," where he emphasized the unmet pledges within our nation's founding documents.

Not keeping one's word has significant consequences. It damages trust, harms connections, and can cause disappointment, betrayal, and resentment in those who depend on them. It also stains one's reputation, making it challenging for others to have faith in and rely on them. This loss of trust can have lasting impacts on personal and professional partnerships, potentially impeding future possibilities. Additionally, failing to fulfill promises can lead to missed opportunities and unrealized potential for oneself and those impacted by the broken commitment. Moreover, it creates a cycle of doubt and suspicion, causing difficulties in establishing collaborative relationships and undermining the overall welfare of individuals and communities.

Many individuals aspire to keep their promises but may require assistance. Often, they attribute their difficulties to external factors beyond their control. Nevertheless, it is crucial to acknowledge that one's thoughts are the only obstacle to fulfilling promises. Recognizing the importance of commitments and exploring any underlying beliefs that may hinder progress is the first step toward achieving this goal. Take a moment to reflect on how not keeping promises affects you personally. Examining and reshaping these thoughts can cultivate a positive mindset that aligns with your dedication to honoring your word. Remember, promises shape our relationships, define our character, and impact the world around us. Embracing the power of keeping promises will strengthen your integrity and contribute to creating a more trustworthy and dependable community.

Riley, could you provide a thorough description of the issue you are currently facing? What specific challenges or obstacles have you encountered concerning this matter? How does it affect your emotional state? To what extent does it impact your daily life? Are there any prevailing beliefs or assumptions you hold about this problem? Do these beliefs limit your progress in addressing it? Have you observed any patterns or recurring themes related to this issue? How does it align with your values and long-term aspirations?

Additionally, are there any external factors that contribute to this problem? Have you attempted any strategies or solutions thus far? If so, what were the outcomes? Can you imagine how your life would differ if you resolved this problem? Finally, do you have any current resources, skills, or support systems that may aid in addressing this issue?

Riley, you have the power to change the impact of empty promises. In this book, I will reveal how God's promises can serve as a solution for those who struggle with keeping their word. These promises include assurance of forgiveness and grace when we recognize our shortcomings and sincerely seek forgiveness. This confidence brings comfort and encouragement in times when we repeatedly break our commitments. By having a relationship with Him, we can experience a transformation of heart and develop qualities such as integrity, reliability, and accountability necessary to honor our commitments. Seeking His guidance and aligning our actions with His will can help us make better decisions and consistently fulfill our promises. This action involves relying on prayer, seeking counsel from spiritual mentors, and studying religious texts to understand and apply His principles. Embracing His teachings can cultivate honesty, humility, and faithfulness within us - strong foundations for keeping our word. Knowing He knows our actions and intentions may instill a greater responsibility to honor our promises.

Above all, God is a faithful promise-keeper. By trusting in Him and His word, you can receive His blessings. He is always reliable and trustworthy in His promises, providing a source of strength for those who have faith. As the Bible says, "The way of the Lord is a refuge for the righteous" (Pr. 10:29). It's like opening an email from a trusted source - you know you can trust both the sender and the message. God's promises are unshakeable and firm; He never makes empty or flippant assurances. Unlike unreliable people who break their promises, God's promises are rock-solid. You can expect Him to follow through because He never reneges on His word. His promises are not only "Yes" but also "Amen." When He says "yes," it truly means yes; you can take that to heart with complete confidence. Do you think God would say yes when He implies no? Not!

His faithfulness never wavers, and Jesus ultimately fulfills all His promises. Therefore, He assures you He always keeps His word.

According to Scripture, God is faithful in fulfilling His promises. He never breaks His covenant or goes back on His word - not even a single word. His promises never fail, so you can always depend on Him and trust His Word. Even in the face of tragedy, life reminds us that no one is immune to its hardships. In those dark moments, we can find our only source of hope in the Lord. We do not turn to cultural trends or clever sayings for comfort; we look to the unchanging character of God. Throughout history, we see how His fulfilled promises have anchored the souls of believers from all generations. From Noah to Abraham to David, and now us, He has remained true to His guarantees without limitation or restriction. When we trace back this unbroken chain of faithfulness to the Old Testament, we find that it all leads to the ultimate fulfillment of salvation through Jesus. Time and time again, God has proven trustworthy by keeping every promise He has made. This assurance solidifies Him as a God of promise - an unwavering anchor for our souls with no weak links.

To receive God's continual blessings and improve your current circumstances, you must cooperate and abide by His conditions. It is a mutual effort. From you, He expects reciprocation. We all desire a better life, and trusting Him brings a sense of fulfillment as He consistently keeps His promises. Keeping promises is vital in building a solid relationship. This book holds valuable information that can bring positive changes if utilized effectively. Through His promises, you can gain insight into His character and personal love for you - faithful, trustworthy, loving, patient, forgiving, kind, and more. He guarantees you a "rose garden." And because these promises are grounded in Scripture, they are yours to claim. You can rely on His Word; it offers immense potential. The context of Scripture makes it clear. Fulfilling

His promises bring honor and uplift others while willingly obeying His will leads to an honest life - my word is my bond.

God has made over 7,000 promises in Scripture, which you can claim in faith. From these promises, I have selected 31 for daily Christian living. In just one month, you can find faith and fulfillment through knowing your responsibilities and how to fulfill them. By immersing yourself in His Word and putting your devotion into action, He'll elevate your faith. The Lord expects us to keep our promises and meet our words. When we make a promise to God, we should quickly fulfill it. God's promises are not flippant or casual; they are solid commitments He accomplishes without fail. His faithfulness is unwavering, as stated in Numbers 23:19. In the Old Testament, there are numerous examples of His unshakable promises:

- This promise, known as the Abrahamic Covenant, pointed to the Messiah for whom Abraham looked (Jn. 8:56).

- There is no hard-to-get God (Dt. 4:29). «Our God is near us whenever we pray to Him» (Dt. 4:7).

- Simple faith reaps the rewards (Ps. 1:1–3)—a blessing for all who delight themselves in His Word.

- According to the New Testament, He promised:

- Give the disciples the gift of the Holy Spirit (Ac. 1:4-5).

- Those who follow Jesus will have abundant life (Jn. 10:10). Following Jesus will bring you more spiritual fulfillment than you could ever imagine.

- He will return for us (Jn. 14:2–3); from then on, we will always be with Him.

While I cannot guarantee a session with Dr. Phil or a genie granting three wishes, you can increase your likelihood of receiving God's blessings by having faith in Him and His promises. Remember, all of His promises are fulfilled in Christ (2Co. 1:20). Finding fulfillment in Jesus should always be your ultimate goal. Remember that His blessings may not always come in the form you expect, but rest assured that He always has your best interests at heart. Stay open to His guidance and ways, and you will experience the fulfillment of His promises. He often confirms His promises with signs, such as when He told the angels to find Jesus wrapped in cloths and lying in a manger (Lk. 2:12). These promises are a source of hope and assurance for you - reminding you of His unwavering faithfulness and love. Take time to reflect on these many promises with trust and gratitude. Allow yourself to be encouraged daily by immediately putting these relevant promises into action. The "right time" for this is now, and here are some steps you can take:

1. Seek a personal relationship with Him: Praying, reading the Bible, and meditating on His word will help you understand His promises and align your life with His.

2. Trust in His timing: He can take a while to fulfill His promises. Patience is crucial, as His timing is always perfect.

3. Obey His commandments: You will receive blessings when you live according to His teachings. Honor Him, love others, and seek justice and righteousness daily.

4. Stay connected to a supportive community: Surround yourself with believers who can encourage and support you.

Having this in mind, you can find faith and fulfillment every month! I have an irresistible deal for you. By fulfilling God's promises, you position yourself to receive His blessings. And the best part is, His promises never fail. So why wait for Him to fulfill them? Take a leap of faith and save yourself from wasting time hemming and hawing. Use this book as your guide to embrace, follow, and act on these promises. Remember that change starts with individual actions. As Martin Luther King Jr once said, "If we wait until we're ready, we'll be waiting for the rest of our lives." Life is precious, so make the most of it now rather than tomorrow. Don't dwell on problems; focus on God's promises instead.

Therefore, decide to open your heart and embrace Jesus as your Savior. It is a significant personal step on your spiritual journey that can bring you peace, joy, and a deeper connection with God. He will never lead you astray. This uplifting devotional offers 31 days of His promises, each day structured into a promise, story of fulfillment, and fruitful application - your daily nourishment. Like Baskin-Robbins' famous "31 flavors," this framework represents a different promise for every day of the month. You can experience His favor for all 365 days of the year. Each month presents a fresh opportunity to immerse yourself in His teachings, conveniently alphabetically listed in the table of contents for easy navigation. Select the most fitting promise that will guide you toward your goal. I designed this book for you to revisit when seeking guidance from His promises and blessings. It inspires and empowers you to put His word into action, strengthening your faith. Unlock the full potential of His promises by embracing them in your life.

Are you seeking to fulfill God's promises to experience growth and change? As a person with vision and dreams, you desire something unique and significant. Above all, His blessings will benefit you greatly. Apply these 31 rock-solid promises and make your life count. They are the perfect start to a fantastic day! Memorize these Bible verses, which serve as a source of strength. Repeating them in your mind encourages you to accept His promises and transforms you by renewing your mind, strengthening your relationship, and drawing you closer to Him. You can live according to His Word and create a new story for your life – Promise. Like the promised land for the Israelites, seek a place or goal that brings success, happiness, or fulfillment. Now that you're ready to dive into this book filled with overflowing blessings feel free to start anywhere you like. I wrote it with that purpose in mind. And if you want to get a head start on the most powerful blessings in Scripture, turn to Day 1 – where it all begins! My friends, declare today that the Lord is your God and walk in obedience to Him. Hold onto His decrees, commands, and laws. Hang on to every word; obedience brings blessings. Yes, Lord – the promise of a new day. You can always count on Him, anchored in His promises.

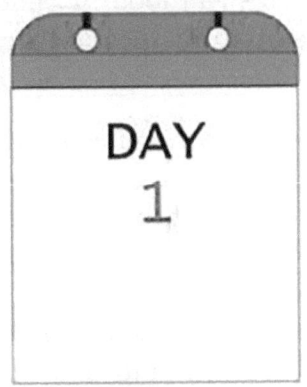

DAY
1

# BURDENS
# (RELEASING DIVINE RELIEF)

*Cast your cares on the LORD*
*and he will sustain you;*
*he will never let*
*the righteous be shaken.*
*Ps. 55:22*

## Delving into the Depth of the Promise

Scripture tells us of this promise's meaning. Whatever your burdens, trials, troubles, crosses, distresses, cares, or fears, you can lay them on his shoulders. *Because* anxiety reacts with fear and worry, the Lord shows concern and acts with reason and empathy to care for your concerns. You can commit to him by faith and prayer and expect a good outcome.

## Fulfilling the Pledge: Honor the Commitment

We all may have experienced the loss of a loved one. A few years ago, The Lord called a beautiful person home to rest. I experienced the unimaginable, devastating, heartbreaking, grief-stricken loss of a first cousin; she was like a sister, and I was at a loss for words. Growing up with my cousin was always a blast; we rode around in her Gremlin, listened to her girls' [Whitney Houston and Janet Jackson] music, and hung out after Friday night football games. She was authentic, caring, warm, and down-to-earth; she had a great sense of humor and the best laugh.

Before going into surgery, she gifted us with her signature laugh and soft smile; she lit up the room. From the love expressed, many others also saw my sweet cousin as a hard worker and faithful friend with a heart of gold. My cousin was a lovely person inside and out; she brought out the best in us. She made us better. I'm sure you have a loved one like this in your life. Though my heart hurt and her loss felt so unreal, I held up and held on to God's promise of strength and sustenance; I pushed send and praised through pain. My cousin will always be in my heart.

Like Ruth and Job, you may have lived through difficult times, too. During Ruth's story, we meet her mother-in-law, Naomi. After the death of her husband and sons, Naomi returned to Israel, and Ruth traveled with her (Ru. 1:1-22). Though discouraged and bitter, Naomi and Ruth had a fantastic bond because of God's goodness. Naomi faced trials and emerged victorious in God's hand.

Similarly, even though Job lost his houses, riches, cattle, and children, he still praised God for his goodness (Jb. 1: 1-21). Job recognized that everything he'd in life came from the hand of the Lord. He continued to *keep* his trust in the faithfulness of God. In the same way, you may have experienced personal heartbreaks like the loss of a family member or close friend or a job or income; you can turn to the Lord for comfort and peace and to strengthen you.

### Embracing the Example: Follow and Act

Is conflict in a relationship or anxiety with your children, job, college, or health your current situation? In each, by faith and prayer, cast your burdens upon the Lord. *Stay* in his assurance, and all will work for your good. You'll feel strengthened by His Spirit sustaining you during your life struggle. Don't worry about anything; pray about everything. God wants to walk beside you through difficult times. He'll maintain, bear up, supply your wants, and satisfy you. When you face trials or tragedies, turn to God.

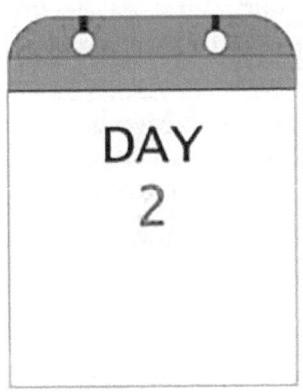

DAY
2

# CHILDREN
# (UNRAVELING HEAVENLY ASSURANCE)

*Children, obey your parents in the Lord, for this is*
*right. "Honor your father and mother"*
*—which is the first commandment with a promise—*
*"so that it may go well with you and that you may enjoy long*
*life on the earth.*
*Ep. 6: 1-3*

## Delving into the Depth of the Promise

When you cast your burdens upon the Lord, he'll carry you in the arms of his power like a nurse cradles a child. Scripture tells us of the meaning of this promise: children obey their parents and honor the duty of parents. Children, obey your parents in everything consistent with your duty to the Lord. In all things lawful, the parent's will be a law to the child. This profound statement is correct, clear, and reasonable. Children should honor (i.e., love, reverence, obey, help) their father and mother.

## Fulfilling the Pledge: Honor the Commitment

I grew up in a Central Texas city that offers a strong quality of life without the typical problems associated with urban growth and development. We have solid values to last a lifetime. Everyone treated each other like family; neighbors were 'extended' parents. Our hood was the 26th Street or 'Purple Jacket' gang. We wore the school colors of a former all-black high school. My siblings and I grew up with solid work, faith, and education ethics. For extra money, we mowed lawns, picked pecans, recycled soda bottles, and caught and sold crawfish for bright and early fishing. I also worked on a small farm where the owner had cows, pigs, etc.

We also went to the store for neighbors; they gave us enough money to buy the item with spare change for a treat. These jobs taught us many valuable lessons about work: integrity, excellence, teamwork, and followership, to name a few. We were encouraged and expected to achieve. Football is king in Texas; some say football is a religion, or Texas is about "God and guns!" We not only looked forward to Friday night football, but we also had a church-going childhood, and school was mandatory. That was the model we had. And if we misbehaved, acted up, or popped off in school, the principal spanked us with a wooden paddle–ouch! Afterward, mama whooped us with a switch, too. And she undoubtedly whipped me into compliance! We understand well children must obey their parents.

The story of Shadrach, Meshach, and Abednego exemplifies an example of obedience and faithfulness. They refused to worship the golden statue of Nebuchadnezzar, king of Babylon. God rewarded their obedience by protecting them when the king threw them into a blazing inferno heated seven times hotter than usual (Da. 3:1-30).

**Embracing the Example: Follow and Act**

Jesus loves the little children who come to Him. We are His kids. We're children of God through faith. His children do what's right and are His heirs and co-heirs with Christ (Ro. 8:17). So, raising and training your child begins with the Bible (2Ti. 3:16). Prayerfully meditate for your children's obedience. Train your children by directing them to the Savior and obeying all God's regulations. The Lord will make you the head, not the tail; you'll always be at the top, never at the bottom (Dt. 12:28). As a parent, if you *keep* obedience to His laws, your children and successive generations, most likely will too. (Le. 25:18).

16

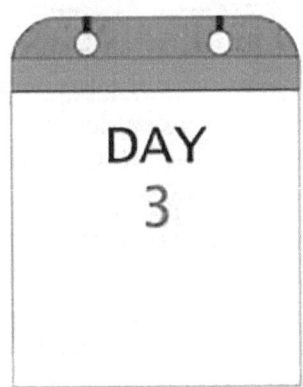

DAY
3

# COMFORT
# (ACCEPTING SOULFUL SOLACE)

*Praise be to the God and Father of our Lord Jesus Christ, the Father of compassion and the God of all comfort, who comforts us in all our troubles, so that we can comfort those in any trouble with the comfort we ourselves receive from God.*
*2Co. 1:3-4*

### Delving into the Depth of the Promise

The Bible tells us children are a reward from God (Ps. 127:3); it's comforting! I hope you're also encouraged by the meaning of God's promise of comfort. He says not to let your heart be troubled. All comforts come from God. Scripture tells us he's as tender as a mother; he comforts us as a mother comforts a little one. Jesus came to this earth to give us hope and comfort. He promised the Holy Spirit would be sent to be our Comforter. In facing loss, we can find comfort and see our loved ones again at Christ's coming. God sends people to comfort you and wants you to comfort others.

### Fulfilling the Pledge: Honor the Commitment

A little girl fell on the sidewalk and skinned her knee. She asked her mother, "Wouldn't it be great if contractors cushioned the whole world?" Unfortunately, our world can be complex, like a rough sidewalk. However, comforted by faith that God is in control, one of my high school classmates shared praise through problems. She first went to the emergency room because of a gallbladder condition, but after a chest X-ray, doctors discovered a spot on her lung. When she followed up with her primary care physician, the doctor referred her to a lung specialist. These pulmonary appointments are usually several weeks out. And it so happened the clinic had an opening that week. She scheduled a lung biopsy, an available appointment usually 2-3 weeks off. Six days later, she had the biopsy and, after 13 days, received her results -- a malignant tumor. After an imaging test, technicians found no other "spots." And then, she had surgery to remove part of her cancerous lung. Though my classmate was the one with bad news, she comforted us by sharing how thankful she was for all God had given her. Doctors didn't leave any stone unturned, and it so happened she's now cancer-free. There will be NO chemo, NO radiation. The surgery took care of it—just surveillance over the next ten years with CT scans. And get a load of this; they only had to remove a "segment" of my lung. Not the entire lung. Not even an entire lobe.

The Book of Psalms put it this way: how God comforted David. He'd escaped for his life from a jealous King Saul and wrote a powerful testimony: "Even though I walk through the darkest valley, I'll fear no evil, for You are with me; your rod and your staff, they comfort me" (Ps. 23:4). Like with David, God is our Comforter in times of trial, anxiety, and hopelessness. Open your heart to comfort the sick, dying, lonely, disheartened, shut-in, defeated, and those who need Christ's love. The God of all comfort comes to you as you pray; seek Him with your heart. He's there when no one else seems to care.

**Embracing the Example: Follow and Act**

Trust God and allow him to *give* you comfort. You sleep when you're comfortable and rested. But, when you face challenging times, you may not sleep well because of discomfort in your Spirit. Despite the situation, believe God will comfort you each day. You can also be comfortable in the uncomfortable when you're in His will. Like Jesus being pleased sleeping in the boat when the storm was all around him (Mt. 8:23-27), you can trust the Lord if you're uncomfortable at work, school, etc.

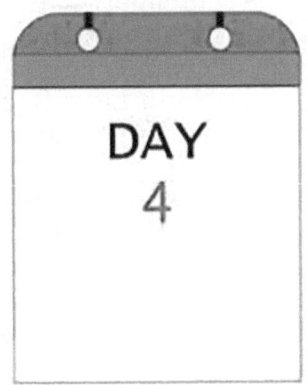

DAY
4

# COMPASSION
## (UNCOVERING SACRED PLEDGE)

*Whoever is kind to the poor lends to the* Lord,
*and he will reward them for what they have done.*
**Pr. 19:17**

### Delving into the Depth of the Promise

While comfort or mercy may refer to God's outward doing in response to sorrow or suffering, compassion denotes inward affection for others deriving from one's heart. His promise of compassion tells us to show concern for the poor, the homeless, the orphans, and the widows. When having compassion and giving to the less fortunate, you alleviate and lessen their necessities and glorify Him. When you enrich people experiencing poverty, you can improve yourself. The Lord takes what's done to them as done to Himself. He has blessed the poor of this world to be rich in faith and heirs of His kingdom (Lk. 6: 20-21).

### Fulfilling the Pledge: Honor the Commitment

During my childhood, I watched my mother cook and take Sunday dinners to friends shut-in and anonymously give money to church families in need. While I served in the active-duty United States Air Force, I continued to show these deep feelings of compassion; I was

19

actively involved in base and community activities. After transitioning from the Air Force and traveling with my active-duty spouse, I sustained the service *of* my heartbeat of compassion and served in the church. At First Assembly of God of North Little Rock (First NLR), where 'Every Soul is important to God,' I show care and invest in others by participating with the homeless, greeting ministries, and other outreach initiatives. In 2015, as one of fifteen teams, my spouse and I served on the Hospitality and Greeters Team. After the meal, I made a blooper when talking with a guest. He had a medical condition and asked for help from potential resources nearby. I was amiss in asking a homeless person, "Where do you live?" He said, "I live under a bridge." My wife wouldn't let me live down my embarrassing slip-up. We led the guest to our prayer team. In short, we helped out with the clothing team the following year.

Lord, we thank You for the many gifts You grant us: a place to live that provides shelter and a roof over our heads, for the sun that shines and warms the earth and our hearts, for the many people who care for us, for life and meeting our needs for food, for family and friends, for times to rest and reflect and pray, etc. Like the parable of the Good Samaritan (Lk. 10:25-37), you can also show mercy and compassion to your neighbors. Scripture also prompts us, "If anyone has material possessions and sees a brother or sister in need but has no pity on them, how can the love of God be in person? Dear children, let's not love with words or speech but with actions and in truth" (1 Jn. 4:17-18).

**Embracing the Example: Follow and Act**

Most don't find giving to the poor or caring for the ill difficult. God commands us to give generously to the poor (Dt. 15:10). Passion also moved Jesus to help a person, even if it was inconvenient (Jn. 11:33). Most folk will feed or pray for the homeless; you can show compassion and take the next step and set up a friendship and aid a life change (Luke 14:13). It's my hope and prayer you continue to connect with God's heart for the poor. Many more areas of society can also foster a compassionate view: civil rights, treatment of animals, or the environment, to name a few.

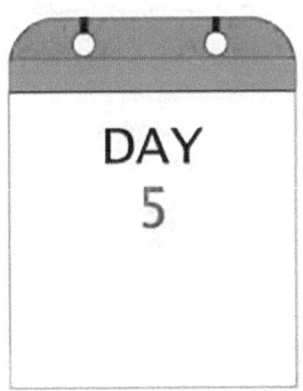

DAY
5

# FAITH
# (INSPIRING SACRED COVENANT)

*"Have faith in God," Jesus answered. "Truly[a] I tell you, if anyone says to this mountain, 'Go, throw yourself into the sea,' and does not doubt in their heart but believes that what they say will happen, it will be done for them. Therefore, I tell you, whatever you ask for in prayer, believe that you have received it, and it will be yours.*
*Mk. 11: 22-24*

### Delving into the Depth of the Promise

A heart of compassion contributes to a heart of faith (Mk. 6:34). Like the inward affection of compassion, faith denotes a direct connection with God. The meaning of this promise speaks of having a robust and firm faith or confidence in the power and faithfulness of God. We're to be fully confident He'll make good his declarations and fulfill his promises in due season. "Now faith is confidence in what we hope for and assurance about what we don't see" (He. 11:1). On this foundation, approach God in prayer. When you fully expect and are sincere, persistent, and decided in asking, you'll receive what you request, as our Lord declares.

**Fulfilling the Pledge: Honor the Commitment**

We can all get antsy about a job raise or promotion. You've been faithful over small things and want to expand your territory and be faithful over more significant things. Faith requires you to "give up something," or you're willing to abandon one thing: the higher the risk, the higher the reward. By faith, my best friend and his spouse put up their house for sale to *move* from Ohio to Alabama, their home state. It took 18 months to sell their house. He possibly gave up a top-level supervisory position after leaving his civilian government job. His spouse moved to Alabama in advance after their home sold, and he began commuting for two weeks. When his partner's medical condition worsened, he asked his boss to telework every two weeks. After his supervisor said, "No," my friend made a dramatic new move to resign. He continued to apply for jobs in Alabama. Once he accepted a job, the Washington DC contractor was unaware my friend had left his government job. My colleague received a telework job where he could work from home, earn the same pay, and *live* nearby for family – Hallelujah!

If you've faith like a mustard seed, Scripture tells us you can say to this mountain, "Move from here to there," and it will move. Nothing will be impossible for you (Mt. 17:20). In the book of Daniel, he influenced King Darius, his employer, to believe in the only true God. (Da. 6:26). By doing a job well in your sphere of work, you can also practically 'show and tell' others with whom you work about Christ. Also, Hannah's plea for a son inspires us to pray and believe (1Sa. 1: 10-11, 19-20).

**Embracing the Example: Follow and Act**

Regardless of your current situation and even when you must 'give up something,' love God with all your heart and mind (Dt. 6:5). The more you think about Him, the more connected you are. He's in your mind, and you can have more self-control over your thoughts. Also, ask Him for help to guide you spiritually. He's faithful to answer. You don't have to have mountain-moving faith; your faith must be present. He will meet you at your level of expectation or faith. Nothing is too hard for Him, and all things are possible with Him.

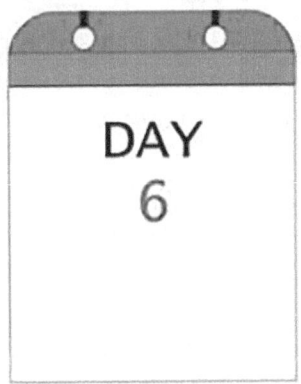

DAY
6

# FEAR
# (WELCOMING SPIRITUAL REASSURANCE)

*I sought the LORD, and he answered me;*
*he delivered me from all my fears.*
*Ps. 34:4*

### Delving into the Depth of the Promise

Fear is the opposite of faith. Occasionally, we refuse to *run* in confidence because of fear. God's promise of delivering us from all fears tells us how David's prayers helped to silence his fears. He sought the Lord, who bore him from all his fears. He *gives* to David not only from the death he feared but also from the worry David was put into by the dread of it. Look unto Him with an eye of faith and prayer and be lifted in comfort and joy. Be secure in the hope of his compassion.

### Fulfilling the Pledge: Honor the Commitment

Despite anxiety caused by the COVID pandemic, finances, debt, recession, conflict and war, the mental health crisis, etc., everybody has a dog story too. Who doesn't love a dog story? I've plenty of stories about Sadie, our former pet beagle, and former family dogs like Champ, Wolfkin, and Buttons. We've always had canines: Lacy,

Coco, Kojak, Nikita, Baker, Jack, Crumpet, Prince, Winston, Bella, and Cojo. I also have a dog story about my past neighbor's full-grown Doberman pinscher. Late one evening, after returning home from a friend's house, I parked my car on the street and began to walk toward my parent's house. They may have turned in early, and the garage doors were down. So, I *go ahead* toward the front door. Then, I caught a flash of white in my peripheral vision galloping from my right out of total darkness, my neighbor's Doberman. Armed to the teeth, they gleamed pearly white. His approach night was "Feed me!" I couldn't beat a hasty retreat to my car, so my M.O. was to get into the house. With leaps and bounds, I pounded the door and hoped my parents had it unlocked. I felt like Casper, the friendly ghost. I was so fearful I wanted to permeate through the door. Then, the Lord –through my mama – delivered me from my fear and opened the door. Thank you, God, for sending Your peace to guard and protect me! He handled it, heard my unspoken prayer, and answered on time! I experienced the fear of being afraid of something – 90 pounds of a meat-eating canine. But I overcame my timidity and had enough self-discipline to reach the front door (1 Ti. 1:7). I then was brave as a lion.

Likewise, I heard about this Sunday morning church service. It was going just fine. All of a sudden, this lightning bolt hit. When the smoke cleared, Satan himself was standing behind the podium. People panicked and ran out of the building as fast as they could. Satan stood there with glee. But suddenly, his mood changed when he noticed a woman sitting in the front row just as calm as can be. He said, "Lady, do you know who I am?" She said, "I sure do." He said, "Aren't you afraid of me?" She said. "No, I'm not." He said, "Why not?" She said, "Why should I be … For 30 years, I have married your brother."

Like the meaning of the promise, Isaiah 41:10 encourages us, "So don't fear, for I'm with you; don't be dismayed, for I'm your God. I'll strengthen, help, and uphold you with my righteous right hand."

### Embracing the Example: Follow and Act

Like these stories, you can also take practical steps to stand on this promise actively: believe God for whatever needs you've. Instability, conflict, lack of peace, and uncertainty can create fear. Fear can paralyze you and cause you to get off the mark; anxiety can result in a fight-or-flight response. Also, fear can separate us from Him as sin separates us from Him. When you trust God, you refuse to give in to anxiety. Being disconnected from Him contributes to tension. You leave your comfort zone and believe in faith rather than fear. You turn to Him even in your darkest times and trust him to make things right. The key to overcoming fear is total and complete trust in Him! If you trust Him, you can't be afraid. Keep faith instead.

DAY
7

# FINANCES
## (UNLOCKING DIVINE ABUNDANCE)

*Bring the whole tithe into the storehouse, that there may be food in my house. Test me in this," says the Lord Almighty, "and see if I will not throw open the floodgates of heaven and pour out so much blessing that there will not be room enough to store it.*
*Ma. 3:10*

### Delving into the Depth of the Promise

Trust in God lessens the fear of having a poverty spirit or a scarcity mindset. This promise denotes bringing the tithe into the storehouse, which were large rooms built for this purpose (e.g., meat, sacrifices, etc.) If lacking, the Lord will supply plenty and, in *part*, to the tithes and offerings you give. Bringing all your tithes denotes paying taxes in full and on time. Strive not to hold back the tithe. In the Old Testament, the law required Israelites to set aside a tenth of all their fields produced yearly. The law also obliged added contributions for the Levites, festivals, orphans, and widows, doubling the taxation to about 23 percent (Dt. 14:28-29). The only place a percentage is required is the old covenant. In the New Testament, honor Him by gladly returning some of the blessings He gives. We have the sacrifice of Jesus Christ.

## Fulfilling the Pledge: Honor the Commitment

It's offering time! Some of you may be wondering why people at church are so excited about the opportunity for giving. I heard about this man. He called the church office and said, "I want to speak to the 'head hog at the trough.'" The secretary was offended. She said, 'If you mean the pastor, you're going to have to call him Pastor, but you may not call him the head hog at the trough.' He said, 'Well, I considered donating five thousand dollars to your church. She said, "Hang on, Porky just walked in."

Feast or famine, my spouse and I faithfully give out of honor for God. When she first became a new believer, she developed a close relationship with a family firm in their Christian faith. One of their encouragements was the concept of tithing. She was a single parent struggling with an Airman's [or first-grade] pay at the time. She felt she couldn't afford to tithe. Her friend lovingly said, "You can't afford NOT to tithe." Her ah-ha moment sealed the deal after she'd tithed, paid bills, and had $70 left for groceries. She clipped at least $20 in coupons and was still $30 short. She carefully chose groceries based on one coupon for each item in the cart. Unexpectedly, the store manager said, "Here, it looks like you can use this." He handed her a $35 voucher! God knew her needs, and he *gave* the way! 's good! Consider too the parable of the talents (Matthew 25:14-30) and shrewd manager (Luke 16:1-14). One master entrusted his wealth to servants when he went on a journey and returned; the other master accused his manager of wasting his possessions. We're also encouraged to use our God-given gifts in his service (1 Pe. 4:10).

## Embracing the Example: Follow and Act

Scripture tells you to have wisdom when managing money like these servants and managers. Know what your expenses are and what income figures you're dealing with. Wise people save or invest for the future (Pr. 21:20). Use good decision-making and control when spending money. Give back to the Lord joyfully, and he'll richly bless you; talk about your stewardship and how God has blessed your faithfulness. Use your money to help others, but with good judgment and His direction. Be wise and a good steward of money. If you carefully follow all these instructions, He will bless you as He promised.

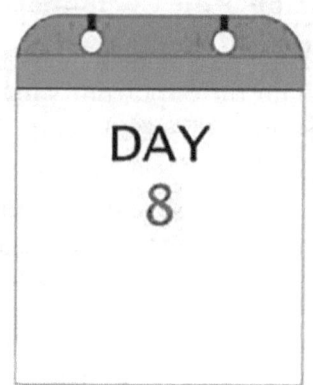

# FORGIVENESS
# (REVEALING REDEMPTION)

*If we confess our sins, he is faithful and just and will forgive us our sins and purify us from all unrighteousness.*
*1Jn. 1:9*

### Delving into the Depth of the Promise

You cannot serve both God and money. The condition of this promise is if you fully acknowledge and confess your sins, He's faithful to His promise to forgive you. He'll do what He's assured: absolving our flaws, faults, weaknesses, or shortcomings. The Lord is upright, denoting He's fair, and His disposition is proper. He will be faithful to His promises, pardoning those who believe in Him. The forgiveness of sins is an act of mercy. You've His word, and He's ready to let you off if you bring to bear true atonement and faith. You can't receive forgiveness without repenting, believing, and confessing. He'll cleanse you from all unrighteousness by forgiving all that's past, known, and unknown. He ultimately removes all the blemishes of guilt from your soul.

### Fulfilling the Pledge: Honor the Commitment

As I watched true crime shows on television, I was astounded not only by the evil of some people but also by the families and victims' forgiveness of murderers. If you spend any time watching actual crime TV, you'll quickly notice the shows always involve one particular type of crime: murder. Often, too, the focus is on exotic, bizarre, and especially grisly or gory details of murder. The killers are glutton for punishment. Like me, at times, you may be one of the millions of people wound up and fascinated by these actual crime shows. God's love is so amazing! Families feel love and compassion and find it in their hearts to forgive; people petition the courts to free the offenders or help them start a new life. They chose not to hang on to anger and revenge. They let go and forgave to help bring healing. Jesus did something special for us when He died on the cross. He canceled a real debt and paid for our sins. Christ took punishment for us. We no longer have debt. He paid it in full (Mt. 27: 32-65).

I also heard about this pastor. He parked in a 'No Parking' zone downtown in a large city. He left a note on the windshield, saying, "Officer, I circled this block ten times. If I don't park here, I'll miss my appointment." In big letters, he wrote, "FORGIVE US OF OUR TRESPASSES." He returned to his car and had a ticket. The officer had written him a note. It said, "Sir, I circled this block for ten years. I could lose my job if I don't give you a ticket." In big letters, he wrote, "LEAD US NOT INTO TEMPTATIONS." We all mess up. The Lord has forgiven you, so you must also forgive (Cl. 3:13). Jesus forgives us for our thoughts, deeds, actions, motives, or heart's intent doesn't align with His word. He's the reason we can forgive others. We love and forgive because he first loved and forgave us (Lk. 23: 33-34).

### Embracing the Example: Follow and Act

Like Jesus' petition on the cross, we should forgive one another as God has forgiven us. In humility, die to self. Jesus also said we're to forgive others "seventy times seven" in response to Peter's question, "Lord, how many times shall I forgive my brother when he sins against me? Up to seven times?" (Mt. 18:21-22). Have empathy for others. Folk can have bitterness or ill will toward you or offend, hurt, lie to, or reject you. We also offend Him every time we sin. So, it's a lot easier to forgive when you remember you need forgiveness too (2Co. 2:5). I'm so glad His grace covers us!

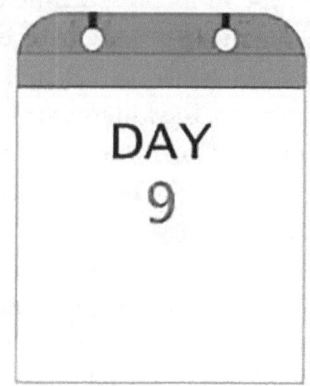

# GODLY LIVING
# (ADOPTING DIVINE GUIDANCE)

*Worship the Lord your God, and his blessing will be on your food and water. I will take away sickness from among you,*
*Ex. 23:25*

### Delving into the Depth of the Promise

Forgiving someone who hurt you is never easy. But with God, it is possible. When you worship and enjoy the Lord, the precept with this promise is his blessing will make your bread and water more refreshing and nourishing than a feast of other things without blessing. He'll take away your sickness; He'll prevent or remove it. He promises where you live won't be visited by widespread, dreadful diseases. He'll fulfill the number of your days. Thus, through Godliness, you have the promise of life now.

### Fulfilling the Pledge: Honor the Commitment

We're all told exercise is good. It is part of being healthy, and the struggle to exercise is real. Like many people, my spouse and I also toil to get enough exercise. I can't count the number of exercise equipment and programs we've invested in; we even converted a bedroom into our 'fitness room.' We recently got another fitness device to propel us to get up and move more. This wearable product changes how we move; it prompts us with hourly messages like "Feed me 250 steps" or "It's step o'clock." My spouse jests, "we're managed" like robots. And it's incredible how much this gadget motivates us. It's not we're addicted to or compulsive about exercise. But, instead of moaning when I've to mow the yard, I excitedly see it as an opportunity to get in lots of steps. To reach our daily activity goal, my spouse and I often burn off steam by jogging or walking in place, jumping jacks, or walking throughout the house like we have an inside track or path. We look to get extra steps in, compelled by the activity tracker. In a sense, the activity tracker "manages" our perspective and motivation.

Is our Christian life different? Paul encourages, "Train yourself to be godly" (1 Ti. 4:7). Physical training may have some value, but spiritual training -- training in Godliness -- is of value both in this life and the next. "Godliness" should be seen as good, clean-living enjoyment of life and God—God-oriented living. Consider the duties to qualify as an overseer or deacon, denoting Godliness in action (1 Ti. 3:2-3, 8). *About* Christians in the church at Ephesus, Paul was steadfast. Healthy doctrine produces healthy deeds (1 Ti. 1:3).

**Embracing the Example: Follow and Act**

Godly people live in such a way as to please God. Godliness is an attitude of seeking to please the Lord. Scripture tells us to live as children of light and find out what pleases the Lord (Ep. 4:17). Godliness isn't avoiding sin to escape punishment. It is avoiding things we know don't please God because we love him more than we love sin or our way. Godliness fulfills the first great commandment: "Love the Lord your God with all your heart and with all your soul and with all your mind and with all your strength" (Mk. 12:29-30). Trust in Jesus and his promises and grow in Godliness.

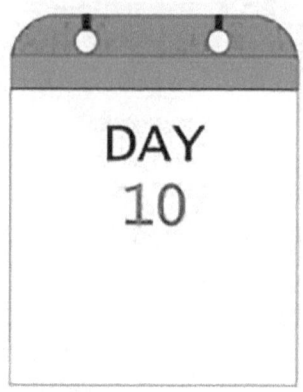

DAY
10

# HEALING
# (UNEARTHING DIVINE RESTORATION)

*He said, "If you listen carefully to the Lord your God and do what is right in his eyes if you pay attention to his commands and keep all his decrees, I will not bring on you any of the diseases I brought on the Egyptians, for I am the Lord, who heals you."*
*Ex. 15:26*

### Delving into the Depth of the Promise

Have faith in God. He'll heal you and promises if you attentively listen to His voice, He'll put none of these diseases (plagues, leprosy, skin, etc.) on you. If disobedient, He'll bear on you the hardships inflicted on your adversaries. Though He implies the danger, He conveys the promise. He is the great Physician --Jehovah Rapha, The Lord Who Heals; the Lord Who makes bitter things sweet. He's your sustainer, *giver*, and comforter. He's your guide, your strength, and your friend. The Lord is our life and the number of our days. He'll heal you, sustaining you in health and healing your ailments.

**Fulfilling the Pledge: Honor the Commitment**

I planned on being home for my brother's surgery. Doctors had discovered a polyp after an exam. Along with family residing in the town, I wanted to be there for my brother and available to help. We talked about how he'd take prescriptions and any help needed, especially since he'd be recovering at home. I stayed at the hospital with my family during the pre-op visit and surgery, which started behind schedule. We undoubtedly welcomed a pastoral prayer for healing before surgery, uplifting my brother's spirit and care. And the good news is my brother made it through surgery after 5 hours and to his recovery room 3 hours later. After an overnight stay, we returned home by noon after doctors discharged him. My brother was happy to return home with his rottweilers.

My brother's speedy recovery reminded me of a story about this 92-year-old man. He wasn't feeling well one day, so he decided to go to the doctor for a check-up. A few days later, the physician saw him walking down the street with a beautiful young lady. And he seemed to be as happy as could be. The medic was surprised. He said, "Wow, you sure are doing much better." The man said, "Yes, doctor, I took your orders. You said to get a hot momma and stay cheerful." The doctor said, "I didn't say that! I said you got a heart murmur. Be careful!" Like the story of h**ealing the royal official's son, you can be confident** Jesus has the power to heal. Jesus healed this man's son without being in the boy's presence. The man believed Jesus would heal his son at his word (Jn. 4:47-53).

**Embracing the Example: Follow and Act**

You, too, can believe, without a doubt, that God will heal when you ask Him. Sometimes, healing may come here on earth or in heaven. Regardless, trust Him for healing and have faith in his supreme will. In due course, our complete bodily healing waits for us in heaven. In heaven, there will be no more pain, sickness, disease, suffering, or death. Strive to be less anxious with your physical state and more alarmed with your spiritual condition. You can then center your heart on heaven, where you don't have to cope with physical struggles anymore.

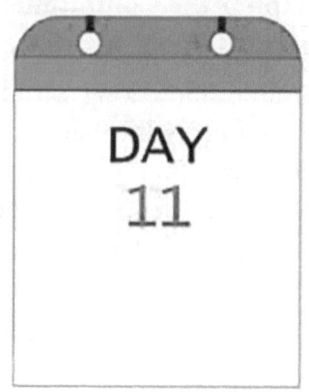

DAY
11

# HOLY SPIRIT
# (ANNOUNCING DIVINE EMPOWERMENT)

*If you then, though you are evil, know how to give good gifts*
*to your children, how much more will your Father in heaven*
*give the Holy Spirit to those who ask him!*
*Lk. 11:13*

### Delving into the Depth of the Promise

Thankfully, God wants to help and heal us — Spirit, soul, and body. The precept with this promise says if you, who's, at any rate, evil and inclined to a needy and pessimistic temper, yet you know how to give good gifts to your children, your heavenly Father will give much more. You should provide what's best and *give* in the best manner and time; present the necessary good. He'll then give you the best and most excellent gift of all, His Holy Spirit; you must sincerely and earnestly ask. Christ encourages fervency and constancy in prayer. It's an essential duty to ask for this gift. Be inspired and believe if you ask right, what you ask won't be in vain. Our heavenly Father is ready to bestow on you all these blessings when you ask for them. For as surely as His power enables him, his goodness certainly inclines him, and his promise binds Him to give the Holy Spirit to you when you ask in the manner; the meaning of this promise points you in the right direction.

**Fulfilling the Pledge: Honor the Commitment**

Many poets used symbolism to deepen the meaning of their poems. In the 7th grade, I wrote my first poem entitled *"An Endless Bondage,"* which also showed symbolism in the following excerpt:

"I feel like a lost person in a world struggling for peace. I feel like a civil rights activist caged from justice. Yet, I know freedom will result from this bondage one day because this bondage is within me."

Writers often use allegory to enrich their writing. We also use symbols to represent everyday life: white represents life and purity. Addedly, we can use objects to imply something else: an olive branch is considered a symbol of peace. Any time something stands for more than its literal meaning, this can be an example of symbolism.

Another example of symbolism is the Holy Spirit, which refers to the third Person of the Trinity (the Father, the Son, and the Holy Spirit); the Holy Spirit is God himself living inside us. Scripture describes it as, "Christ in you, the hope of glory" (Cl. 1:27). So, we receive the Holy Spirit by receiving the Lord Jesus Christ as our Savior. Also, in addition to names and titles, other symbols that refer to the Holy Spirit are fire, rest, sacrifice, oil, wine, water, dove, and wind; they're signs of new life.

**Embracing the Example: Follow and Act**

As you meet a bewildering variety of symbols each day, let's remember the Spirit's presence as the dove at Jesus' baptism symbolized the gentle Savior bringing about peace to humanity through His sacrifice (Mt. 3:16). As a believer, the Holy Spirit already dwells within you and isn't a million miles away. You can be continually filled (Ep. 5:18) with the Holy Spirit by daily spending time in prayer and Bible study (Ac. 4:31) and obeying His commandments (Jn. 14:15).

DAY
12

# HOPE
# (FORESEEING ETERNAL ASSURANCE)

*Be strong and take heart, all you who hope in the Lord.*
*Ps. 31: 24*

### Delving into the Depth of the Promise

God, the source of *hope*, will fill you with joy and peace because you trust Him. Then you'll overflow with confident *hope* through the power of the *Holy Spirit* (Ro. 15:13). When you're of good courage, you're encouraged to be strong, namely, in the Lord, and through confidence in his promises; they won't fail you. The Lord will strengthen your heart. Trust Him, and He'll pass on resilience and endurance to you. Lord, pardon our complaints and fears; increase our faith, patience, love, and gratitude. Teach us to delight in difficulty and hope. Put your hope in Him; rely on Him for grace and glory and to supply all your wants. When you hope in Him, you've reason to be of good courage and strengthened. Nothing genuinely evil can come about you, so He'll withhold nothing perfect from you.

### Fulfilling the Pledge: Honor the Commitment

We all like to celebrate starting anew. "Even with holiday festivities, 'Jesus is the reason for the season,' and look forward to next year and his and our story getting even better!" That's usually our signature closing for our *MO2-4L Praise Newsletter,* celebrating our year in review. When spending time with family in Texas during the holidays, another part of our M.O. is watching college bowl games. One of the most memorable national championship college games I ever watched was the 2006 Rose Bowl Game. It featured the only two unbeaten teams: the defending Rose Bowl champion, Texas Longhorns, against the two-time defending national champions, the University of Southern California Trojans. The highly expected matchup was a back-and-forth contest; Texas secured the victory (41-38) in the game's final 19 seconds on a fourth down and five yards to go for a first down.

Gideon is also a textbook example of an underdog. Scripture tells us the Lord gave the Israelites into the hands of the Midianites for seven years because of their evil ways. When the Israelites cried out to the Lord because of Midian, he turned to Gideon to go and save Israel out of Midian's hand. This story is so hopeful because all things are possible with Him. He thinned down a force from 22,000 to 300 men, and Gideon defeated an army of 135,000 Midianites. The victory was the Lord's; God received the glory. (Jg. 6-7).

### Embracing the Example: Follow and Act

Like Gideon, keep hope, even if the possibilities appear hopeless. You can have the victory as long as God is on your side. You can anchor your hope in his word and promises. Numbers don't matter with God. When we've him, we're the majority. Similarly, you can also have hope like Nehemiah. Though the task may be excellent, the workers few, and the haters many, what's done in God's name and for God will succeed and prosper, bringing him glory (Ne. 1-6).

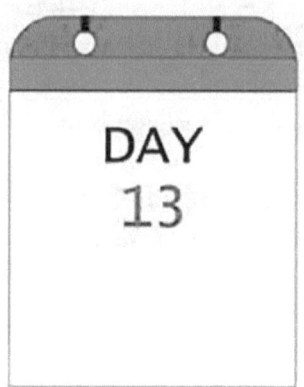

**DAY 13**

# HUMILITY
# (EXPLORING HUMBLED BY GRACE)

*For those who exalt themselves will be humbled,*
*and those who humble themselves will be exalted.*
*Mt. 23:12*

**Delving into the Depth of the Promise**

Believers can show the world the hope they have inside through joyful, humble readiness to endure offenses and serve. How reasonable are the conditions of this promise when you humble yourself and lift others? Will God reward your humility? The Pharisees prescribed conformity to the Law of Moses. Pride was their ruling sin; it plagued them to appear as fanatical hypocrites and more religious than others. They demanded respect, and their titles puffed them up. We may judge according to external appearance, but God searches the [inward] heart.

**Fulfilling the Pledge: Honor the Commitment**

When I had my chief master sergeant pin-on ceremony, I felt humbled by the occasion as a measure of success and an opportunity to help others more. The moment of being chosen for promotion to chief master sergeant, the highest enlisted rank in the US Air Force, was a dream come true and a blessing; it was one of the happiest days of my life. Besides passing on 'words of wisdom,' the recognition is primarily an opportunity to share your gratitude. Like others, during the occasion of promotion and retirement, I'd a host of people to thank who lent a helping hand: God Almighty versus Lady Luck, the chaplain, senior leaders and supervisors, my commander, chiefs, mentors, friends, my Airmen, family, facility location, co-workers, and peers, and attending audience. My eyes were wide open to the blessings given me, and it was so natural to express my gratefulness with a humble heart. The privilege of leading others gives you the humility that uses the words *we, team,* and *us! The* honor of leadership allows you to put other people first.

Scripture describes the Pharisees' behavior as arrogance instead of humbleness. They did everything for people to see and for show (Mt. 23). Contrast the Pharisees' brazen conduct with Jesus' humility. He was born in a lowly barn, he put others before himself, and he never bragged. His servant leadership guides his followers. John the Baptist also encourages us to be humble, testifying about Jesus, "He must become greater; I must become less." (Jn. 3:30). Along with Jesus and John the Baptist, Paul is an excellent example of humility. He saw himself as the "least of the apostles" and the "chief of sinners" (1Co. 15:9).

**Embracing the Example: Follow and Act**

Everybody wants to be humble; nobody wants to be humbled. God has promised to show favor to the humble while opposing the proud (Pr. 3:34). For that reason, come clean and put away pride. Avoid taking credit, admit your mistakes, learn from and praise others, go last, help others succeed, or serve someone. If you put yourself on a pedestal, you conflict with Him, who will humble you in His grace and for your good. But when you humble yourself, He gives you more favor and elevation.

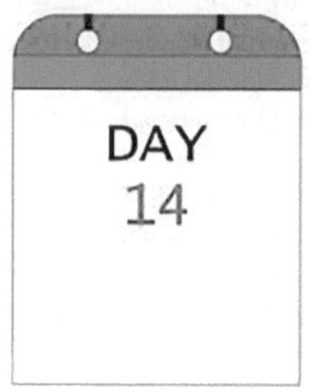

DAY
14

# JUDGMENT
# (UNDERSTANING OUR IMPERFECTIONS)

*"Do not judge, or you too will be judged. For in the same way you judge others, you will be judged, and with the measure you use, it will be measured to you.*
*Mt. 7:1-2*

**Delving into the Depth of the Promise**

Nothing may change you as much as the humility in striving to understand instead of judging others. The principle of this promise is you mustn't self-judge and shun making our word the law to one and all. You mustn't think hastily or pass judgment upon each other without merit or foundation. We should see the best in folk. Judging can hold you back from godliness. Our Lord's words imply evading passing judgment harshly and critically. Sidestepping assumes people without full, clear, and specific know-how of their fault or behavior and with an attitude of love. To be not judged with harshness, don't judge others. If you assume considerately, making proper allowances for folks' weaknesses, showing concern, and letting go of their faults, God and man will take care of you likewise. And with what measure you allot, he'll share with you. So, it's up to us whether or not we're dealt with hard-heartedly or graciously.

**Fulfilling the Pledge: Honor the Commitment**

As a retired chief master sergeant, being a military spouse in Guam was a new role. My role as a key spouse accompanied my spouse's duty position as a command chief. As a key spouse, I supported the base commander's spouse expectations; she advocated the leadership team extend chiefs' spouses as part of the wing leadership team. I was blessed to be a part of a team, and I'm grateful to our chiefs' spouses' team again for their volunteerism and service! When we arrived at the base in November, the chiefs' group and their spouses had welcomed my spouse and me at our home. We hit the ground running, firstly meeting with spouses at base events. To help form the team and build rapport, I suggested a first spouses' potluck social at our on-base home in early December. Well, several of the male chiefs were vocal about their spouses attending the get-together. We make judgments every day. In this case, the emphasis may have been on getting together with spouses too soon instead of with chiefs and their spouses, which happened months later. As a last-ditch stand, I worked with another chief's female spouse to help bring the event together. This opening helped fortify the chiefs' spouses to support Airmen and their families at Team Andersen. The Bible declares a two-faced way of thinking is wrong (Mt. 23). Isaiah also prophesied about hypocrites: "These people honor me with their lips, but their hearts are far from me." (Mk. 7.6).

**Embracing the Example: Follow and Act**

Scripture tells believers against judging others dishonestly or wickedly; Jesus commends "right judgment" (Jn. 7:24). You must be discerning and talk about God's whole purpose and will. You're to gently deal with fellow believers who slip up and care enough to speak the gospel into the lives of those around us. Judgment belongs to God.

# LOVE FOR ENEMIES
# (CLARIFYING DIVINE LOVE)

*But love your enemies, do good to them, and lend to them without expecting to get anything back. Then your reward will be great, and you will be children of the Most High, because he is kind to the ungrateful and wicked.*
*Lk. 6:35*

### Delving into the Depth of the Promise

Mercy triumphs over judgment (Ja. 2:13). How rich are the particulars of this promise to show compassion and generosity? If you lend, you don't have to be afraid or awed; you'll lose what you give. Give with a resolve to lose it, but overcharging is forbidden, and stealing is prohibited, especially without cause. When you see people reduced to lack and cannot pay interest, you should show love and mercy like the example of our heavenly Father.

### Fulfilling the Pledge: Honor the Commitment

As a part of our polarized culture, two core American values — freedom of religion and freedom from discrimination — continue to clash. Pitted against each other are religious freedom believers who oppose same-sex marriage and LGBT [lesbian, gay, bisexual, and transgender] supporters; they discriminate because their sexual orientation is prohibited. When listening, viewing, or reading what's happening in the news or blogs, you may have also heard these back-and-forth stories: from Chick-fil-A's anti-LGBT activism, the right for same-sex couples to marry, announcement transgender people won't be allowed in the military; or a baker who refused to sell a wedding cake to a gay couple. In the military services, we also emphasize people will treat all with dignity and respect while all *stay* focused on doing assigned missions. Similarly, when Jesus said we're to love our enemies, he upped the standard for relationships -- the law of love. The second commandment tells us to love our neighbor as ourselves, yet it doesn't imply you should hate your enemy. Jesus declared we should love our enemies and neighbors (Jn. 13:34-35).

Let's go ahead and admit it: living up to this expectation seems impossible! For better or worse, a few folks may feel you're "enemies." They seem to hate on you. If you've offended them, they reject your expression of regret regardless of your actions. You may have upset coworkers, or they may be haters; they've set themselves against you. Family members may hold a chip on their shoulder against you for whatever reason. For example, I heard about this man. He was on vacation in Jerusalem with his family when his mother-in-law suddenly died. He went to plan to get her body back home. The consulate said, "It would cost $5,000 to have her shipped. But he could have her buried in Jerusalem for $150." The man thought about it a moment and said, "I'd like to have her body shipped home." The consulate said, "Wow, you must have loved your mother-in-law." The man said, "Naw, it's not so much that. I remember this case many years ago when they buried somebody, and on the third day, they arose. I can't take that chance."

Some people may dislike you; you can't change them, and letting go is utmost. Even though your nemesis acts like a jerk to you, you don't have to conduct yourself like a jerk toward your foe.

### Embracing the Example: Follow and Act

No matter your opponent's actions, open your heart to them and act toward them with kindness; choose to love them (Mt. 5:44). Jesus realized that a sincere example of love grows out of a constant and total yielding to God. Love grows into an action rather than a feeling. And pray for them, too. Pray for Him to transform their hearts by the Holy Spirit. Walk out love for enemies by living out Day 8 (forgiveness), seeing the goodness in your adversary, and searching for their understanding. So, what's pronounced is hard, but it's not impossible. With Him, all things are possible.

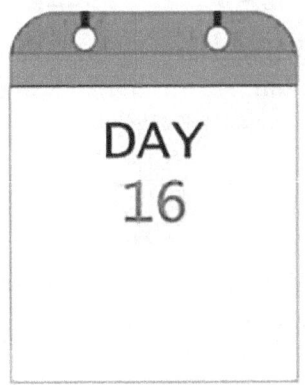

DAY
16

# MARRIAGE
# (TAKING UP A SACRED COMMITMENT IN THE SCRIPTURES)

*Wives, submit yourselves to your own husbands as you do to the Lord. For the husband is the head of the wife as Christ is the head of the church, his body, of which he is the Savior.*
*Ep. 5:22-23*

### Delving into the Depth of the Promise

Marriage is for people who love their enemy. Throughout your lifetime, your spouse will be your best friend and, sometimes, your enemy. But, if you love your spouse during calm times and uproar, you'll have victory in your marriage. The cherished belief linked with this promise proposes wives yield to their husbands except where God prohibits it. Husbands must love their wives. Both sides will have letdowns and shortcomings, which doesn't alter the association. He includes all the duties of marriage in unity and love. You have Christ's authority in your husband, whose image you bear. A wife exhibits compliance with her husband as she reveres Christ himself. The husband is the wife's guardian, as Christ is the head of the church. In such a way, the husband should apply his influence over his wife.

**Fulfilling the Pledge: Honor the Commitment**

Our culture perceives marriage as a relationship that can drain the life out of you or make you feel miserable. You may have heard of this view in TV shows like "Married with Children," "The Old Ball and Chain," "Kitchen Pass" labels, or bachelor and bachelorette parties as the "last chance" to have fun before you give up your freedom. God's intent is for marriage to be fulfilling. He designed and created marriage as a good thing -- a beautiful, priceless gift. You may have had a childhood vision of what marriage should look like. Some married couples have unrealistic expectations of their bridal and each other.

Like this husband I heard about, in this situation, you may undergo trials and challenges in marriage. He was quietly reading his newspaper when his wife snuck up behind him and hit him in the head with a frying pan. He said, "What was that for?" She said, "was for the piece of paper I found in your pocket with the name Mary Lou on it." He said, "Aw honey, that's one of the horses I bet on at last week's racetrack." She apologized and went about her business. Two days later, she hit him on the head with a bigger frying pan. When he came, he said, "What in the world was that for? She said, "Your horse called."

You can make it through with God as your source and first strand in your marriage. Folks can't quickly break a cord of three strands [God, husband, and wife] (Ec. 4:12). Gain great comfort from his word and design of a husband-and-wife unit (Ge. 2: 18, 22-24). Scripture tells us of great, genuine love marriage relationships: Adam and Eve, Mary and Joseph, Abraham and Sarah, Jacob and Rachel, and Ruth and Boaz.

**Embracing the Example: Follow and Act**

Jesus must have loved weddings. His first miracle took place at one. Regarding some of His analogies, He described His relationship to the church in wedding terms. You also want to enjoy life and enjoy your marriage. Learn to trust and lean on God and His word. I hope you and your spouse continue to grow in understanding each other in a spirit of oneness and unity. As you walk in the fruits of the spirit of love, joy, peace, patience, kindness, gentleness, goodness, faithfulness, and self-control, you'll receive profound revelation and knowledge to apply to your marriage day by day.

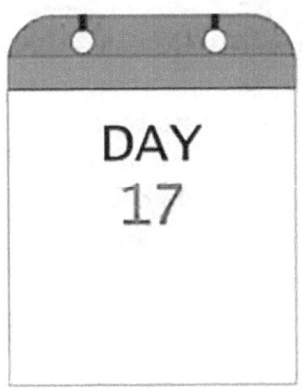

DAY
17

# NEARNESS
# (ILLUMINATING DIVINE PROXIMITY)

*What other nation is so great as to have their gods near them
the way the LORD our God is near us whenever we pray to him?
But if from there you seek the LORD your God, you will find
him if you seek him with all your heart and with all your soul.
Dt. 4:7, 29*

### Delving into the Depth of the Promise

When drawing nearer to God, you can realize the beauty in marriage He intended for you. He exemplifies his nearness by his wonders, grace, promises of his presence, and principally by his readiness to hear our prayers. Considering our many appetites and our heart's unethical wants, carefully guard your heart. Let's clasp to our faithfulness by love and cleave to Him. Your prayer success depends upon your faithfulness. Scripture tells us: "Come near to God, and He'll come near to you." (Ja. 4:8) and "Return to me, and I'll return to you" (Ze. 1:3) (Ma. 3:7).

### Fulfilling the Pledge: Honor the Commitment

It's a family thing! Though I was excited to be out of the country for the first time in 1985 during my first 12-month overseas assignment in the Republic of Korea, I still felt a little lonely. There's no time like a joyful season spent with family and friends. Firstly, I resolved not to embrace the Korean culture. My base sponsor appealed to me for the first three months to 'get off the yard' and visit the local villages and nearby cities. That Christmas, I was on duty in a locale many of my friends couldn't pinpoint on a map. Operating as a detachment during an isolated remote assignment at Pilsung Range, also known as the Korean Tactical Range, may have added to the loneliness. Also contributing to the isolation was that most members lived and worked in the same building. In addition to the seclusion, winters were bone-cold, and there were about 45 Airmen and 250 Korean Airmen -- all men! When I finally "got off the yard" and explored the new culture and colorful scene, I overcame being homesick by drawing near to Korean traditions; yet there's no place like home.

When Adam and Eve chose to disobey the command of God, their sin also caused them to withdraw from the nearness of God; sin separates us from God. (Ge. 3: 6-10). The Exodus was also a time when God set himself apart from all other "gods." He distinguished Israel by his presence. Also, Jesus was the One who left His home to draw us to Himself. His people looked to a future day when they entered an intimate communion with Him – His omnipresence and nearness!

**Embracing the Example: Follow and Act**

The rest of the Bible is about the plan and purpose of God to deal with man's sin so we can again enjoy fellowship with Him in his presence. When I finally "got off the yard," home is always near because it's where I'm from and who I am – an ambassador for Christ. And with Jesus, I'm never alone. Likewise, He is ever near in the sense he sees and hears what men are doing -- "His Nearness." Talk with him, live by his decrees, repent, and allow his Spirit to dwell in your heart and mind. Draw near to Him, and he'll draw near to you (Ja. 4:8).

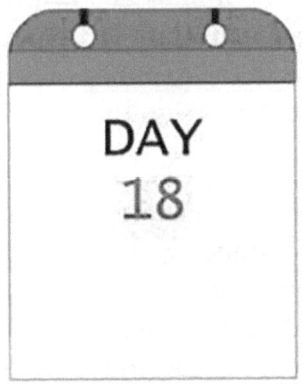

DAY
18

# NEW LIFE
# (ACHIEVING RENEWAL AND REDEMPTION)

*Therefore, if anyone is in Christ, the new creation has come:*
*The old has gone, the new is here!*
*2Co. 5:17*

**Delving into the Depth of the Promise**

But as for you, the nearness of God can be your good; you can make the new life in Christ your refuge (Ps. 73:28). The direction connected with this promise says His real followers exist in Him in place of themselves; they divinely know Him and become His servant by being alive in devotion and residing in His Spirit. As a new believer, his sense of right and wrong is progressive, stimulated, and stands apart from wrongdoing by Jesus' blood. He exposes Jesus' will to His will. All old man views and habits pass away. The new man acts upon fresh values with new ends. Though the same man, he's transformed in character and conduct. He's new, godly life.

**Fulfilling the Pledge: Honor the Commitment**

Deciding to join the military was my first career decision. For the next twenty-six years, I lived 'a great way of life,' as the Air Force recruiting slogan promoted. After basic military training in San Antonio and technical training school in Wichita Falls, Texas, The Air Force assigned me to 11 permanent duty locations. They included three places in Texas, two sites in the Republic of Korea, and two locales in Washington, DC, Japan, Germany, Turkey, and Florida.

I was also temporarily assigned to the following spots: Panama, Italy, England, Belgium, Macedonia, and throughout Germany, including the former East Germany. Addedly, I've traveled as a tourist throughout the Pacific and European theaters in countries such as the Philippines, France, and Bulgaria. Also, as a spouse supporting my wife when she was on active duty, permanent duty locations included assignments in Georgia, Guam, and Arkansas. Having served over half of my life in the military, this 'great way of life' was also a 'new way of life,' which began in Air Force Basic Training in San Antonio, Texas.

Many Bible characters also have had to start over or begin again: meek Moses from prince to fugitive to shepherd to leader (Ex. 2-6); Gideon from hiding to hero (Jg. 6-7); Esther from orphan to Queen (Es. 1-2); David from teen shepherd to King of Israel (1Sa. 16); and the heroes and heroines in the Hall of Faith (He. 11:32-39).

**Embracing the Example: Follow and Act**

Like the champions of faith, you, too, can receive your reward now because of your faithfulness. You understand God cannot lie, and He'll deliver the promise at the right and proper time. You can also be the following story of a new beginning. Also, he's the Father of second chances and third chances and beyond. You can make a new beginning, and if you've not asked forgiveness and believed in Christ, then begin there. Like beauty and the beast, you can still make a new life in Him. Come to know Christ personally, put away the old self, be renewed in the spirit of your mind, and put on the new man.

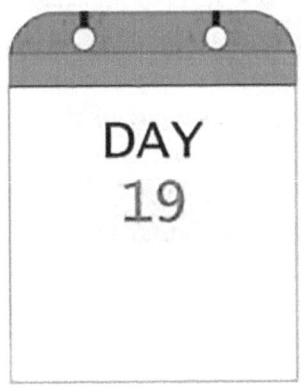

**DAY 19**

# OBEDIENCE
# (WALKING IN HARMONY WITH GOD'S WILL)

*Whoever has my commands and keeps them is the one who
loves me. The one who loves me will be loved by my Father, and
I too will love them and show myself to them."*
*Jn. 14:21*

### Delving into the Depth of the Promise

Come near to God, and He'll come near to you. Wash your hands,
you sinners, and purify your hearts, you double-minded (Ja. 4:8). The
first verse of this promise points out the continual steps leading up to
His whole appearance. The first step is a moral concern and everyday
adherence to His decrees. The unquestionable proof of our love for
Him is to obey His laws. *About* one's love for Him, the next step reveals
the Father exclusively loves the believer. When a follower's heart shows
genuine love to Him, obedience will trail. In the third step, the Son's
extraordinary love shadows the Father's special love and goes along
with the Son's whole appearance.

### Fulfilling the Pledge: Honor the Commitment

It's important to obey traffic laws when driving. At a time, I used
to be pretty lead-footed. During my active-duty Air Force days, I

51

remember two occasions when traveling to different cities where I got pulled over and ticketed, not once, but twice. Aargh! As most motorists stopped for speeding, though *called for*, I'd rather club-wielding police not issue a ticket. In a try to get out of the ticket, I wish I'd the wit of this senior citizen I heard about. He was cool as a cucumber. He was driving down the freeway in his brand-new Corvette with the top down, going 80 miles per hour, when he saw flashing red lights from a state trooper in his rearview mirror. He floored it and took off at 100 miles an hour without thinking about it. He heard the sirens behind him. He finally pulled over and said, "Officer, I'm so sorry; I don't know what I was thinking." The state trooper said, "Listen, it's Friday, 4 o'clock, and my shift is over in 30 minutes. If you tell me why you're speeding, I've never heard before, I'll let you go." The man thought about it and said, "Officer, years ago, my wife ran off with a state trooper, and I thought you were bringing her back." The officer said, "Have a great weekend!"

Though obedience is easier said than done, you can find encouragement from others who have done that. In Jesus Christ, we find the perfect model of obedience. He lived a sinless life. As His disciple, we follow His example as well as his commands; our motivation for obedience is love (Jn. 14:15). King Saul also turned away from following the Lord's commands (1Sa. 15:22). Also, the story of Noah shows he obeyed Him (He. 11:7)!

**Embracing the Example: Follow and Act**

Obedience is tough. It becomes a contest when we feel lured to believe we stand to lose more through our obedience than we might gain. You may have to be dutiful to a boss, parent, crack troop, or traffic law. Obedience is a part of our faith that comes from our submission, giving in, and compliance with God's will; we continually apply our faith. Living out faith on Day 5 required "giving up something." In obedience, you give up your will, control, and trust; your life becomes Christ-centered versus self-centered.

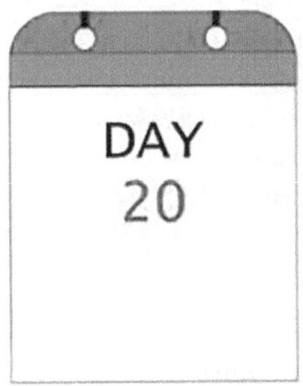

**DAY 20**

# PATIENCE
# (TRUSTING IN GOD'S PERFECT TIMING)

*Let us not become weary in doing good, for at the proper time
we will reap a harvest if we do not give up.*
*Ga. 6:9*

### Delving into the Depth of the Promise

*Stay* on the course Christ has set through your obedience; wait on Him despite all obstacles and trials. The facts of this promise are splendid. With an outlook of joy, let's not be weary or discouraged in well-doing. No matter what work and exhaustion, whatever expense and difficulty, cope with it. You'll reap in due season when the crop comes or when it's suitable with Him. Expect an abundant harvest if you stay strong. Give your best according to your ability, at any time or place, and in any way you can. Do well in every possible way and to all men, especially believers.

### Fulfilling the Pledge: Honor the Commitment

How many of you like to fish? It's not a baited question. Sure, some ladies like angling, but by a show of hands of your husbands or guy friends, "How many know they're a good fisherman? Hit me up on Facebook; I'd like to talk with you after reading this. I love fishing;

I love to eat fish. I don't claim to be a good fisherman, but now and then, when you throw your line out and reel in a big fish, you want to say, "Thank you, Jesus! Hallelujah. Thank you, Lord," "Yeah," or whatever expression suits you. There was a joke about fishing I was going to tell you. Oh no, I forgot the line! The gentle hint I'm about to write to you'll shock you – fishing requires patience.

While in Japan, our men's fellowship group went fishing at a fishpond. One young boy saw a big redfish swimming near the pond's bank. He quickly baited his line and put the bait before the fish. So, fisherman, "What do you think happened next?" The fish swam away. We want things Like fast food, service, and solutions now. The young boy re-tried this bait-and-hook technique for 10 minutes and finally gave up -- hook, line, and sinker. You'll also be encouraged by Abraham and Sarah's faithfulness and Job's patience.

Abraham and Sarah's impatience evoked them to take matters into their own hands to produce a child, Ishmael. Yet, God fulfilled his original promise by the birth of Isaac through Sarah when Abraham was 100 and Sarah was 99 years old (Ge. 17: 1-15). While impatience, like Abraham and Sarah's, can sometimes have long-term effects, Job was best known as a person of patience. Thus, the common saying is, "The patience of Job." Job showed patience to continue to trust God. Job waited for God's answer to Job's trials (Jb. 1:8-22).

**Embracing the Example: Follow and Act**

Patience is a virtue and requires a little wait. Like fishing and Abraham and Sarah or Job, patience does bring about suffering on some level – whether boredom, being childless, or facing trials. Even as we wait, God reveals His will to us and works all things together for our good and His glory. When you go through tough times of testing, you often don't see why He allowed it to happen until a later time. Patience isn't a weakness. It shows great strength, especially when exercised on behalf of others.

DAY
21

# PEACE
# (FINDING SERENITY IN GOD'S PRESENCE)

*Do not be anxious about anything, but in every situation,
by prayer and petition, with thanksgiving, present your
requests to God. And the peace of God, which transcends all
understanding, will guard your hearts and your minds in
Christ Jesus.*
*Ph. 4:6-7*

### Delving into the Depth of the Promise

If you want peace, an inner feeling of calmness, you must also want patience. Patience and calm go hand in hand. The lead-up to this promise inspires you to be careful of nothing. Those who agonizingly worry may expect to feel alone and self-reliant among life's problems and risks. Let believers be of one mind and ready to help each other. Pray on all occasions with all kinds of prayers and *asks*. Prayer and supplication with thanksgiving generally denote worship. Though different, they're attached. The peace of God, the calm feeling of being reconciled to Him and having His favor and blessings, sustains you from weariness. This calm before the storm will cling your heart and mind to Jesus Christ, the Prince of Peace. This type of harmony comforts you in your times of trial.

**Fulfilling the Pledge: Honor the Commitment**

After a return trip from Texas to Arkansas, I was approaching the outskirts of Little Rock when I met a motorist on Interstate Highway 30 on her cell phone. I needed an opportunity to pass to follow the vehicle. It's unclear what made the driver slam on her brakes, but she may have perceived I interrupted her morning talk or texting. As for me, I may have had the "Drive friendly, the Texas Way" attitude. I interpret this saying as moving out of the left lane when sitting at the speed limit, which blocks others from passing. When the opportunity became available, I passed the vehicle to get ahead of the driver. Looking back in my mirror, she displayed non-verbal motions, weaved in and out of traffic, and exited the highway. I'm glad we could keep half of our peace and not throw arrows. We didn't lose our peace or reach for crabs at the bottom of the barrel. Folk can hold their peace and bury the hatchet by talking versus arguing, being the bigger person as a giant instead of a small person or hero versus zero, or rising above as an eagle instead of a crow. I strived to give peace in place of power and be a champ for God rather than a chomp for men.

Similarly, I heard about this man at the airline ticket counter, hollering and screaming at the agent for being so rude. As he continued to rant and rave, the agent was just as calm and polite as possible. She treated him so respectfully like it didn't even bother her. He left, and the next man stepped up and said, "Wow! I am so impressed. You must be a Christian. How could you possibly be so kind to him?" She smiled and said, "Aww, it wasn't that hard. He's going to Detroit, but his bags are going to Bangkok."

In the book of Acts, James was a role model for keeping the peace when the apostles and elders met to consider if the Gentiles must be circumcised and required to keep the Law of Moses (Ac. 15: 5, 6, 13, 19). His compromise of non-circumcision and abstinence offered a peaceful solution and gained the apostles' consensus.

**Embracing the Example: Follow and Act**

The point of this scripture is we can achieve peace through understanding. James dealt with a possibly contentious issue like a roadmap to peace instead of road rage, brought about peace, and honored God. In this instance, let's encourage others to embrace the peace and harmony they, too, can feel with Him. Can you change the things you don't like about the world and still be enclosed in calmness? Can you accept the world as it is while still trying to change it? Rest in Jesus' presence and receive peace. Let the peace of Christ rule in your hearts (Cl. 3:15).

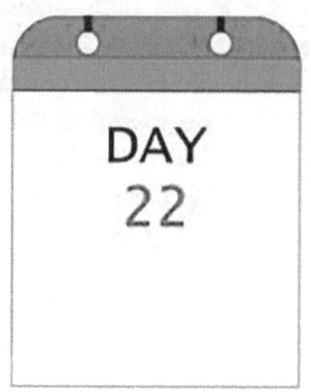

**DAY 22**

# PRAYER
# (UNLEASHING THE POWER OF PRAYER)

*Ask and it will be given to you; seek and you will find; knock and the door will be opened to you. For everyone who asks receives; the one who seeks finds; and to the one who knocks, the door will be opened.*
*Mt. 7:7-8*

### Delving into the Depth of the Promise

Lord, make me an instrument of your peace. The encouragement covered by this promise guides you to ask God for supernatural aid. Ask, as a beggar asks you to donate. Ask, as a traveler asks directions. All are welcome to the throne of grace when you come in faith. Seek help from Him in all problems; this promise covers a critical path and reassuring appeal. Search for a thing of value you've lost or as the businessperson pursues goodly treasures. Seek, and you'll find. When you knock, persistently endure in your work, and your efforts won't be in vain. Knock, as one wants to enter a house, knocks at the door— like I knocked at the door on Day 6. As long as you ask what's acceptable to His will and in harmony with his laws, He'll give to you. Everyone asks to receive His goodness and faithfulness, especially believers.

Whatever you pray for, according to the promise, He gives to you if He sees it suitable for you.

**Fulfilling the Pledge: Honor the Commitment**

Often, I see a post on social media with someone asking, "Please pray for so-and-so" for an individual facing an ailment or some hardship. Many people comment on the post, such as "Prayers being sent your way" or "Praying." When sending a prayer, do folk pray, especially if the recipient is a stranger? Do they intend to pray or mask feeling good about themselves? Do they believe random, heartless prayers will fulfill their *ask*? Is "keeping the person in your thoughts" a more sensible response? Others note they *ask* and pray on the spot or during the time they devote daily. Giving the help of the doubt, I'm encouraged by the member *ask*ing for prayer on someone's behalf. They offer such a prayer in faith; they believe in and relate with God and feel he hears and responds to prayers.

The earnest prayer of a righteous person has great power and produces excellent results. Consider, for instance, the answered prayer of Elijah and Jesus. Elijah first blessed a widow and her son by amazingly causing her food not to run out (1 Ki. 17:7-15). Later, he prayed for the child's life to return to him, and God answered immediately (1 Ki. 17:21-22). Elijah also prayed earnestly that no rain would fall. None fell for three and a half years! Then, when he prayed again, the sky sent down rain, and the earth began to yield its crops. In the night, Jesus was betrayed and arrested. He pleaded with His Father to avoid the torture and death he knew awaited him. He ended his prayer with a statement of complete obedience to God: "...not as I'll, but as you'll." His ultimate want was to do what God wanted, which is the part of the prayer God answered. (Mt. 26:39). Calvary covered it all; that's so good!

**Embracing the Example: Follow and Act**

So, when others ask for prayer, they believe God will answer prayer, even if the answer is "no" or "not yet." Regardless of the answer or timing, He always listens. You can also embed prayer in your life by setting up a time, place, and method for prayer.

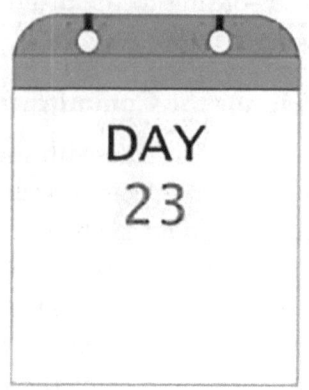

**DAY
23**

# PROTECTION
## (APPLYING THE DIVINE SHIELD)

*Whoever rests in the shadow of the Most High God will be kept
safe by the Mighty One.
He will cover you with his wings. Under the feathers of his
wings you will find safety. He is faithful. He will keep you safe
like a shield or a tower.*
*Ps. 91:1, 4 (NIRV)*

### Delving into the Depth of the Promise

A prayer for God's hedge of protection: "I run to you, Lord, for
protection. Don't disappoint me" (Ps. 71:1). The principles of this
promise are when you make God your dwelling and sanctuary, you'll
abide by the Almighty's shadow, which signifies he protects. You rely
on him in your dangers and difficulties and live a continual relationship
with Him. Choose Him as your protector by faith and find all you need
or can want in Him. You'll find a quiet and safe relaxing place under
his divine care. Believers may comfortably know they're under the
same almighty Protector. He'll protect you with the greatest love and
warmth. And under his wings of overwhelming power and wisdom,
He'll be your shield. His shield is the very highest. His defense is solid
and sure. He promises excellent security to believers in danger.

**Fulfilling the Pledge: Honor the Commitment**

It was an early Saturday morning. I was returning from holiday leave in my hometown in Central Texas to my first duty station in San Antonio. I was eager to return to Kelly Air Force Base because the weather and roads worsened. The roads were slick, and it was forecasted to begin snowing hard. Like many of my fellow safe drivers, the thought of driving in winter can cause crushing, knee-knocking, unbearable fear – at least in the back of your mind. One thing stops because many people have no experience driving in snow and ice conditions. So, the driver's fear is even though you know how to maneuver in those extreme conditions, it doesn't mean you're safe. My driving appeared to get better after entering onto the interstate highway. After first skidding, my driving on ice slowed down to a crawl, and the snow continued to fall as I headed south. In Round Rock, a driver swerved from another lane and caused me to brake hard. To add insult to injury, my 1981 Monte Carlo and I slid off the road and down into an entrenched ditch. At the time, concrete barriers didn't separate the interstate expressway. I walked to a nearby grocery store and called home. My mama and dad, an Army veteran more skillful in driving in icy conditions, came from home, picked me up, and safely transported me to Kelly Air Force Base. I'm so grateful for my parent's undying love and protection!

I also love the comfort and Bible stories like baby Moses (Ex. 2: 1-10), Esther (Es. 4-8), David and Goliath (1Sa. 17), and Daniel (Da. 6), which speaks of God's protection.

**Embracing the Example: Follow and Act**

I hope these fulfillment stories encourage you to be in your "safe place." Wherever you seek safety, God is present with you in that place, which *gives* you the strength and protection you need. Honor Him and do what's right; you can trust the Lord for protection. He's your Shepherd. He'll take care of you, and you'll not want (Ps. 23). Stay in the herd -- a part of His family and receive His protection. His angels will encamp around you.

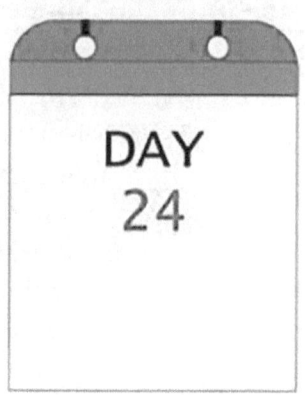

## DAY 24

# PROVISION
# (GATHERING THE ABUNDANT ASSURANCE)

*So don't worry. Don't say, 'What will we eat?' Or, 'What will we drink?' Or, 'What will we wear?' People who are ungodly run after all those things. Your Father, who is in heaven, knows that you need them. But put God's kingdom first. Do what he wants you to do. Then all those things will also be given to you.*
*Mt. 6:31-33 (NIRV)*

### Delving into the Depth of the Promise

By spending time in God's presence, you're inviting Him to pour out His blessings to protect and *give* in your life. In this promise, you're fortified not to worry *about* how He'll *give* for you during your lifetime. Prune ungodly distraction, separation, anxiety, or unbelief, for your heavenly Father knows your needs. He has promised food and clothing, and you may expect them. Don't worry about tomorrow. Don't worry about the things of this life and become preoccupied with them. Seek first His kingdom. When you're in short supply, the whole matter is to trust Him for your daily needs. Your worries will fade once you understand how much He loves you. Learn to turn your fears or cast all your anxiety over to Him.

## Fulfilling the Pledge: Honor the Commitment

It was an uncomfortable situation. I've been in *"transitional seasons"* multiple times where the resources I used to see come in to help *give* abruptly died out (e.g., retirement, relocation, etc.). Now, I was in between banker's hours jobs again. I looked forward to conversing with my wife; it was a talk we'd to iron out. Better late than never. Familiar with songs like Gwen Guthrie's "Ain't Nothin' Goin' on but the Rent" and Destiny's Child's "Bills, Bills, Bills" didn't ease the approach. For better or for worse, life always seems to present you with opportunities. My spouse and I hammered out a promise to get through this together as a part of moving forward. Job loss made money tighter, and we trusted Him for provision. Like when I first transited from the military and *move*d to a new city, I'm so grateful for my service to the country, and my retirement pay helped fill the gap. It's not a fickle fortune and thank Him for his blessings! In 5 months, I burned the midnight oil and applied for 64 cutting-edge information technology jobs, interviewing for ten jobs before landing my current position. Thank God for daily providing!

Similarly, I heard about this minister who asked for protection yet became a provision. He was out bear hunting. He searched through the woods but saw no sign of a bear. Finally, in frustration, he threw his gun down and went down to the stream to cool off. About that time, he saw this large grizzly bear racing toward him. He knelt and said, "Please, God protect me. I'm asking God to convert this bear into a Christian." Miraculously, the bear froze, put up both paws toward the Heavens, and said, "Thank You, Lord, for this food I'm about to eat." Learning to trust God for daily providing reminded me of the Prophet Elijah's experience. Soon after Elijah voiced God's decree of a dry spell in Israel, God sent him to a desolate place where God used the Ravens to supply Elijah bread and meat daily, and he drank water from the brook (1Ki. 17:1-5). See Day 15 for God's provision for Elijah, the woman, and her family (1Ki. 17:1-15). Food for thought: they were likely hungry as wolves.

## Embracing the Example: Follow and Act

Jehovah-Jireh, "The Lord Will Provide," will generously *give* all you need. Then, you'll always have everything you need, and plenty left over to share with others. As believers, even in the "dark times," our dependence and hope come from the Lord. God can bless you abundantly as he used ravens and a widow to *give* for Elijah. Whether a check in the mail or a financial gift received at the right moment, you can depend on Him. Everything is under his command, and He *gives* what's needed and when needed. God is your source.

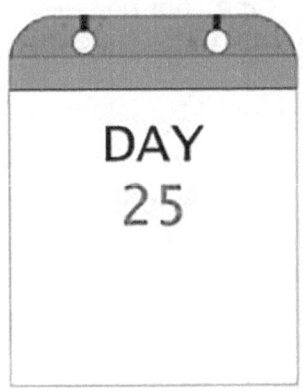

DAY
25

# REPENTANCE
# (EXPLORING THE DIVINE INVITATION)

*"But if a wicked person turns away from all the sins they have committed and keeps all my decrees and does what is just and right, that person will surely live; they will not die. None of the offenses they have committed will be remembered against them. Because of the righteous things they have done, they will live.*
*Ez. 18:21-22*

### Delving into the Depth of the Promise

Repentance influences our behavior; it motivates us to obey God's commandments and accept His provisions for salvation. Claim this promise over your life; if the evil person will turn from wickedness by repenting, he'll surely live. God can save a wicked man if he turns from his sinful ways. The word repent means to feel regret, turn from your sin, and turn to Jesus Christ for forgiveness. He'll not assign to wicked men the way they transgressed in the past. In the righteousness which the wicked has done, he'll surely live. God will divert the penalty and forgive. He won't reveal or credit the evil person's wrongdoings on him; they'll be as if they were gone. The Lord wants to save all men and for us to understand the truth. He doesn't want anyone to perish. True believers watch and pray and continue to the end. And The Father saves them.

## Fulfilling the Pledge: Honor the Commitment

Many couples throw mud at money, sex, work, parenting, and housework. Rather than become a grace giver versus a rock thrower, most argue about these five burning issues repeatedly; these irritants speak to our sense of love and regard. In the end, an offense leads to one of us apologizing to the other for an action. You want to back up the "I'm sorry" instead of smoothing over things, whitewashing, avoiding the real issue, getting out of jail free, manipulating, or getting off the hook. However, I heard about this middle-aged woman who didn't sincerely want to change. She had a heart attack. On the operating table, she asked God, "If this was it?" He said, "No, you have 40 more years." Upon recovery, she decided to stay in the hospital and have a facelift, tummy tuck, and liposuction -- an extreme makeover. Two months later, as she was leaving the hospital, she was hit by a car and killed. She got to heaven and said, "God, I thought you said I had 40 more years." He said, "I'm sorry. I didn't recognize you."

For when Jesus forgave the woman caught in the act of adultery (John 8:1-11), a change or repentance is required to deserve forgiveness. *Like* a child breaking house rules or a criminal being arrested, He said, "Go now and leave your life of sin." To admit you erred, a change in heart is also needed (2Co. 7: 9-11). Otherwise, the offender may violate again. Like John the Baptist (Mt. 3: 1-6), Jesus preached repentance rather than speaking of an apology. He talked about a genuine change of heart. Unlike the apologies of athletes and politicians or Bible characters like Pharaoh, Balaam, or Judas, David turned to God and genuinely repented. It is to God we must turn for help, and it is against Him we've sinned.

## Embracing the Example: Follow and Act

What David told God applies to us, too. By repentance, you can obtain forgiveness of sins and enjoy fellowship with Him. He uses his people, like Nathan, to confront people with their sin (2Sa. 12:1). Like Zacchaeus (Lk. 19:1-9), repent and grow. Pray the Father makes you aware of your heart and opens your eyes to repentance. Genuine apologies can happen only when you take responsibility for your behavior, acknowledge the other's point of view, and make changes. If applicable, change your lifestyle and behavior. Only He can change hearts. In this regard, repentance is His work. By repenting, you can confess your flaws and your dependence upon Jesus Christ himself. You change your mind, and the mind change leads to a change in your life.

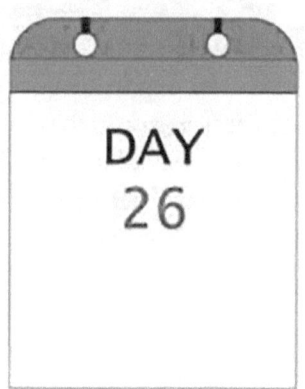

DAY
26

# REST
# (COMPREHENDING SERENITY AWAITS)

*"Come to me, all you who are tired and are carrying heavy loads. I will give you rest. Become my servants and learn from me. I am gentle and free of pride. You will find rest for your souls. Serving me is easy, and my load is light."*
*Mt. 11:28-30 (NIRV)*

### Delving into the Depth of the Promise

"In repentance and rest is your salvation," says the sovereign Lord (Isaiah 30:15). Review His promise of rest with trust and gratitude. Those who work hard are weary and burdened. Come to the Father. Specifically, this promise refers to those who are tired of Satan's bondage, the world's love and search for its pride, life's distresses, and various trials, and want His resolution, peace, and rest. While waiting to enjoy these blessings, people may become heavily laden with blame, iniquities, and His discontent. When you come to Him as The Father, you must recall He's Lord of heaven and earth; go to Him with reverence as the sovereign Lord of all. Draw near to Him confidently, as one able to defend you from evil and supply you with all good. In coming to Christ, you petition Him in faith and prayer for such blessings as you want. And He alone will freely give you rest as a gift: from anger and the useless guilt and power of sin; worldly likings, cares, anxiety, and sorrows; trials and life's troubles. You have His Word. Everything will work for your good, and you'll have peace and comfort in your heart and find rest for your soul.

## Fulfilling the Pledge: Honor the Commitment

You may spend 100,000 hours working in your job over a lifetime. The words "work" and "toil" are mentioned over 480 times in The Bible, supporting the importance of work to God. Work is so essential. In Exodus 34:21, He commands, "Six days you'll labor, but on the seventh day you'll rest." Similarly, the Merriam-Webster Dictionary defines retirement as "withdrawal from one's position or occupation or active working life." Your culture may promote the goal of retirement as ceasing all labor to live a life filled with leisure. You may have 'retired,' but you want folk to think you're in no way tired. I heard about this 85-year-old woman. She went on a blind date with a 92-year-old man. She came home frustrated, and her daughter said, "Mom, what's wrong?" She said, "I'd to slap him three times." The daughter said, "You mean he tried to get fresh?" She said, "No, I thought he was dead." Growing older, you still use your talents and skills to help others.

Like the words "work and toil," "rest and relax" is a repeated theme throughout Scripture, beginning with creation week in the Book of Genesis. God created for six days; then He rested. He set the standard for humanity to follow (Ge. 2:2-3). The Ten Commandments made people resting on the Sabbath a *need* of the Law (Ex. 20:8-11). And now Jesus is our Sabbath rest. We can rest in Him always instead of 1 day per week.

## Embracing the Example: Follow and Act

Most of us don't think of taking on anything huge when we reach a certain age. But you can still do great things for God, no matter how old you are. He wants rest for us because it doesn't come naturally to us. Get your rest and trust He will take care of things for you. When He refreshes you and you're capable, you can finish the work He has called you to do. He'll *give* you the needed strength. Instead of being put 'out to pasture' or feeling "weary and burdened," draw near to Him, and He'll give you rest (Mt. 11:28).

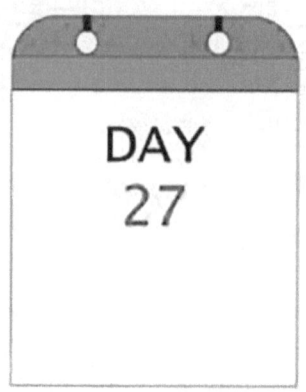

## DAY 27

# RESURRECTION
# (DISCOVERING RISEN GLORY)

*"Do not be amazed at this. A time is coming when all who are in their graves will hear his voice. They will all come out of their graves. People who have done what is good will rise and live again. People who have done what is evil will rise and be found guilty.*
*Jn. 5:28-29 (NIRV)*

**Delving into the Depth of the Promise**

The rest of the dead didn't come to life until God ended the thousand years. This reign is the first resurrection (Re. 20:5). In this promise, you'll discover God will do what He's promised. If you hear His word and believe He has everlasting life, He will not condemn you. The hour is coming and has now come when everyone in the graves will hear the Son of God's voice and live. He'll present those who were dead in sin to the newness of life. The Lord will then raise the dead in their graves. He declared His authority and character as the Messiah. He's all knowledge, almighty power, and 'last word' to judge. By faith and hope, believe His testimony so you repent and don't come into blame on that grave day.

## Fulfilling the Pledge: Honor the Commitment

Only some days you get the chance to start something over again. The good news is there are second chances, new starts, or resets. Every day can be a fresh start to a brighter day. Like many veterans transitioning into or from the military service, one of my resets was shifting to civilian life again. Some people may have been high school dropouts or drank too much and got popped. Other individuals may have had the wrong major in college or hurt or screwed over a friend. What we've learned in hindsight is that all were platforms for learning and growing from our mistakes. You can't turn back the hands of time. One of my wife and I's favorite TV shows is *"Dancing with the Stars."* In the finals, a couple will choose a dance style for their redemption dance; the last time *they did it,* they likely received their lowest score. In an irony of fate, the judges typically reward the couple with a higher score for their redemption dance.

Consider, for instance, the second chances of Bible characters raised from the dead, like the blessed event of Jesus' Resurrection:

- Elijah raised the widow's son (1Ki. 17:17-24)
- Elisha uplifted the Shunammite's son (2Ki. 4: 20-37)
- Jesus upraised a widow of Nain's son (Lk. 7:11-16), a synagogue ruler's daughter (Mk. 5:35-53), and Lazarus (Jn. 11:1-44)
- Peter elevated Tabitha (Ac. 9:36-41)
- Paul lifted Eutychus (Ac. 20:7-12)
- God raised many holy people upon Jesus' death (Mt. 27:51-53)

Similarly, Jesus died and rose again. Death was powerless to hold Him in the grave. The second coming of Jesus Christ is soon (Jn. 14:1-3). Stay woke! He'll then raise to life the righteous dead and along with the moral who's still alive on the earth (1Th. 4:16-17).

## Embracing the Example: Follow and Act

When you trust Christ's blood, you can be sure you'll have eternal life with Him. You have the assurance of salvation, a blessed event.

Because He died, you're given the gift of "second chances" and can resist wrongdoing, grow in obedience, and love others as He loves you—glory to God for the power of Christ's death.

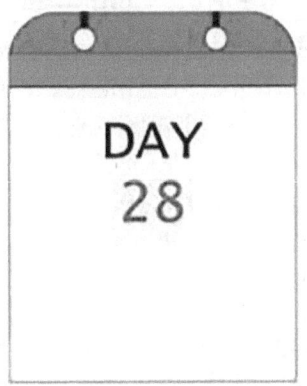

DAY
28

# SALVATION
# (UNCOVERING ETERNAL REDEMPTION)

*If you declare with your mouth, "Jesus is Lord," and believe in your heart that God raised him from the dead, you will be saved.*
*Ro. 10:9*

### Delving into the Depth of the Promise

Jesus' death and Resurrection are central to believers and their salvation. In Genesis 3:15, the Bible records the first promise of salvation. The rest of the Bible is how God fulfills this promise of salvation so sinful men can again draw near to Him. In this promise, you'll explore its meaning: believers don't oppose confessing with their mouths and believing with their hearts. You can view each as the essential result and expression of the other. You can regard each as equal in acknowledging Jesus as Lord. We must devote and give up our souls and our bodies to Him: our souls in believing with the heart and our bodies in confessing with the mouth. In being raised from the dead, Jesus was delivered over to the Grim Reaper for our sins and raised to life to identify our flaws. As spelled out on Day 27, the proof of Jesus' promise and expectation would have been incomplete without the Resurrection. His death wouldn't have had its saving worth and value.

**Fulfilling the Pledge: Honor the Commitment**

While visiting family in Texas for the Thanksgiving holiday weekend, a church teaming up with local businesses to feed travelers touched me. They served the annual meal at rest stop areas on both sides of the interstate highway. *Like* the story of Jesus feeding 5,000 people with a loaf of bread and two fish (Mt. 14: 19-21), the team could freely feed over 600 families and members. They didn't ask guests to drop money in the bucket; it was all a gift.

Salvation is also a gift. God has given us eternal life in His Son, Jesus Christ. In other words, the way to *have* eternal life is to through His Son. There are no deeds for you to do; He did it. A guy asked Rick Warren, an American evangelical Christian pastor and author, "What can I do for God to save me?" Pastor Warren said, "You're too late! You're about 2,000 years too late! What He needed to do for your salvation, He has already done it, and you can't do anything about it. He paid for your salvation on the cross, and it's now your gift. That's why when He was hanging on the cross, He said, "It is finished." He didn't say, "God is finished with me," because God wasn't. He's still alive today. The "it" is your salvation. He finished the plan to *give* you grace (Ro. 3:24).

**Embracing the Example: Follow and Act**

I hope you value the price He paid at the cross. Salvation is His gift; it's the greatest gift someone will ever offer you (Jn. 3:17). Comparable to saving for your favorite vacation spot or bucket list adventure, Jesus is worth it! This gift is the good news of the Bible: God's own Son who became a man, lived a sinless life, died on the cross for our sins, and was raised from the grave. He promised salvation to all who believe in His Son (Ro. 1:16–17); He promises eternal life (1Jn. 2:25). There's no more tremendous blessing than the gift of His salvation; it's all a gift!

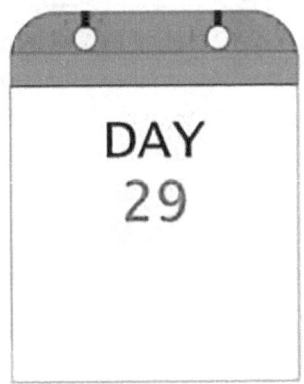

DAY
29

# SUCCESS
## (SORTING OUT DIVINE PROSPERITY)

*Never stop reading this Book of the Law. Day and night you must think about what it says. Make sure you do everything written in it. Then things will go well with you. And you will have great success.*
*Js. 1:8 (NIRV)*

### Delving into the Depth of the Promise

Once you've accepted Christ as your savior, pray regularly, read the Bible, and get plugged into a local church. Success is developing a more profound, personal relationship with Him. Proclaim this promise over your life encourages you with His promise and presence. Constantly meditate on His Word by reading the Bible. Diligently study it daily, keeping with His will and your duty. *See* to do according to what's written and understand it. By obedience and faithfulness, all will go well when you speak the Word. You'll make your way prosperous and have success.

### Fulfilling the Pledge: Honor the Commitment

As a retired Chief Master Sergeant, I often share words of wisdom with Airmen about career success. Airmen seek guidance from a guy who started at the bottom and rose to the top. In my 26-plus years in the Air Force, I've encountered many people with their secrets, pillars, or keys to success; you need more than a "magic formula" to achieve a successful career in today's Air Force. Your career is what you make it. The great thing about the military is that the thing you need to be successful is right there in front of you. If you want to attend school, use tuition assistance and available programs. If you wish for the Air Force to promote you, study for promotion, and do what it takes.

*Like* this promise of reading the Book of Law, I was busy as a bee. I planned, read, highlighted, dissected, memorized, *show*ed, studied, and critically studied our professional development guide to help prepare for my promotion test. The Air Force selected me for promotion to the coveted award of chief master sergeant. I charted a course to career success and helped others to grow and prosper. Comparable to reading the promotion guide, ponder, for instance, these other verses about reading the Bible. Ezra, the priest, read from the break of day till noon (Ne. 8.3). Scripture also tells us faith comes from hearing Christ's message (Ro. 10:17). Since Jesus is the Word, folk must listen to the Word by speaking it for people to hear about faith in Christ. God inspires Scripture (2Ti. 3:16-17), and his Word will achieve what He sent it out for (Is. 55:11).

### Embracing the Example: Follow and Act

We could efficiently devote more energy to self-improvement methods. New and growing believers should learn sooner rather than later. When you're off at the start and travel that path, you can be off by miles later. Read through this promise verse by verse; reading it aloud brings God's Word to life. His Words are alive, active, powerful, and inspiring. When you memorize His Words, you can draw on them like Jesus when tempted in the wilderness by Satan (Ps. 119:11). His Word will help defend you when tempted or tested. He'll carry you through severe trials. Read it, use it, and you'll love it. Success is being faithful, one moment at a time, by honoring Him with an attitude that pleases Him. Like Joseph (Ge. 39:2), stay steadfast in every moment. Success always leaves footprints.

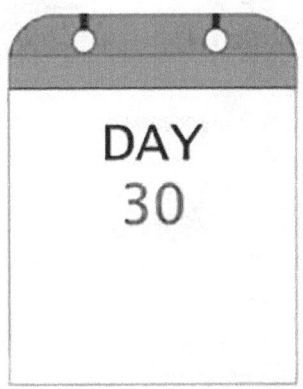

DAY
30

# TEMPTATION
# (BUILDING SPIRITUAL FORTITUDE)

*You are tempted in the same way all other human beings are.*
*God is faithful. He will not let you be tempted any more  you*
*can take. But when you are tempted, God will give you a way*
*out. Then you will be able to deal with it.*
*1Co. 10:13 (NIRV)*

**Delving into the Depth of the Promise**

Consider when folks tempt you with success. Decide to trust God, and you can resist temptation. But this promise encourages you that you're able to bear temptations every day or suited to man. He *allows* the temptation by allowing the conditions that enable enticement to arise. With each temptation, He makes a way to escape from it. He'll make your burdens according to your strength. He knows what you can bear. He is faithful. Be fully encouraged to flee from sin and to be faithful to Him. You cannot fall by temptation if you cleave fast to Him.

**Fulfilling the Pledge: Honor the Commitment**

I heard about this lady who was shopping with her husband. He asked her not to buy any new clothes. Well, she saw this dress in the window and decided to try it on; she liked it so much she bought it in secret. A couple of days later, the husband discovered it. He was so upset. She explained to him when she tried it on, it looked so good, Satan tempted her to buy it, and she couldn't resist it. He said, "Why didn't you do what the Scriptures said and say, 'Get behind me Satan?'" She said, "I did, and he told me it looked even better from a distance."

Though you may know about the enticement of Jesus (Mt. 4:1-11), Sampson and Delilah (Judges 16), and David and Bathsheba (2Sa. 11:1-4), among other Bible characters, this incident makes me *show* on Adam and Eve yielding to Satan's original temptation (Ge. 3:1-7). Satan is crafty and deceptive, not straight. Like Eve, his pattern for typically tempting us allows our inner yearnings to relate to the world's lures. He recognizes temptation is most potent when you're all alone and tests you on the authority of God's Word, character, and judgment. Also, Satan intrigues you with the possibility of gratification but doesn't allude to the glaring omission.

Like Eve saw the fruit, the lady shopping saw the dress as a delight to the eyes. It looked as if it would meet a real need, either sex or comfort. And the results seemed firstly beneficial. Hopefully, her *buy* didn't alienate her from her husband like Adam and Eve's sin led to them separating from one another and God. If temptation and sin defeat you, He *gives* the way of deliverance.

**Embracing the Example: Follow and Act**

God doesn't leave you alone. Like the story of Joseph and Potiphar's wife, you can resist and flee temptation by focusing on Him (Ge. s 39:9). He gives you a way out. Stay steadfast in living with a mind to please Him even when alone; you can resist Satan's devious charms. Satan is a personal adversary; pray, rebuke, and cast down. Jesus will deliver you from evil spirits and his forces of darkness. Pray, and He'll answer your prayers and grant you the strength to persevere in faith and resist every temptation. Don't be deceived by what you see, hear, or feel. Stand on the truth. Be alert, *stay* on guard, and stay firm in your faith when you're undergoing temptation or sorrow.

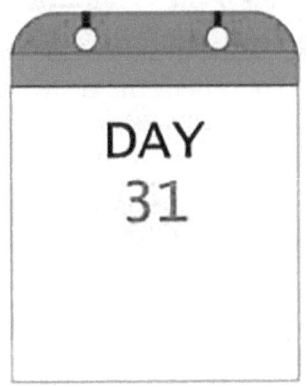

**DAY
31**

# WISDOM
# (IGNITING THE TIMELESS GUIDANCE OF SCRIPTURE)

*Trust in the Lord with all your heart.*
*Do not depend on your own understanding.*
*In all your ways obey him.*
*Then he will make your paths smooth and straight.*
*Pr. 3:5-6 (NIRV)*

**Delving into the Depth of the Promise**

God is faithful; He'll not let others tempt you beyond what you can bear. But when folks entice you, He'll also *give* you a way out so you can endure it (1Co. 10:13). Last but not least, the promises' conditions are, if you trust in the Lord with all thy heart, lean not on your understanding, and in all ways acknowledge Him, He'll make your ways safe and sound. Rely on His wisdom, power, and goodness, and promises for direction and help in all your affairs and dangers. Trust in the Lord with all your heart. He's able and wise to do what's best. You acknowledge Him by knowing Him; you follow His directions, expect success from Him, and manage your activities in a way that pleases and glorifies Him. He promises He'll direct your paths.

**Fulfilling the Pledge: Honor the Commitment**

Many students ask, "What'll I do after high school?" For some, the answer is "get a job." For others, the answer is "to travel and see the world or to continue education." I decided to 'continue my education' at a local college before enlisting in the United States Air Force to 'see the world.' My decision immediately resulted in gratefully serving my country; my service continues to be a blessing in disguise! But I obligingly experienced many second and third-order consequences, which were different yet directly linked to my first decision: permanent change of station or assignment, unaccompanied tours, temporary duty including short or no-notice deployments, alerts, recalls, extended hours or shift work and the real possibility the government would call me to make the ultimate sacrifice in the line of duty.

The people of Judah also stood at a crossroads and on the cusp of a significant decision when God inflicted their nation with disaster. He promised them two things: He'd restore their land if they stayed in Judah or death, or they'd leave this life if they went to Egypt. They decided to 'pitch their tent' in Egypt; they made a choice based on their wisdom and direction versus God's, and they eventually passed away (Je. 42: 8-22). At Gibeon, Solomon also made a wise decision when he asked Him for wisdom (1Ki. 3:5-12). Wisdom and understanding are essential gifts He gives us. When you decide to have faith in your life and do it in obedience to Him, The Lord will always lead you down the right path. He is with you.

**Embracing the Example: Follow and Act**

As you face your own tough, essential decisions, remember to look to God's Word to find wisdom for that situation (Ja. 3:17). You can gain insight by fearing and obeying Him rather than disobeying Him. When you walk in relationship with Jesus, He'll guide you in knowledge and understanding to build your life on the solid foundation of His wisdom (Mt. 7:24). Praise Him for ordering your steps and instructing you how you should go. As you follow Him, your path will become more apparent each day.

# CONCLUSION

## *Embracing Jesus: A Journey of Acceptance and Transformation*

In conclusion, Riley, let's take a moment to review what we've discussed. You've read this book and explored the significance of keeping promises and the repercussions of breaking them. Whether it's a New Year's resolution or an advertisement that falls short, people often need help to follow through on their promises. You aspire to fulfill your commitments, but sometimes doubts or external factors can sway you. It all begins with a thought, which turns into a decision and, ultimately, an action. When you don't honor your word, both parties can feel disappointed – the one who promised something and the one who made the promise. Breaking a promise can lead to feelings of worthlessness, sadness, rejection, and inadequacy. But fear not; there is a solution: trust in God's promises. When you vow to Him, it is essential to keep your word and not procrastinate in fulfilling it.

Trusting in His promises can bring hope, guidance, and transformation to your life. Relying on His promises involves:

- Developing a deep and intimate relationship with Him.

- Seeking His guidance.

- Surrendering your will to His divine plan.

Believe in the unwavering faithfulness of God, even when facing challenges or shortcomings. His promises are a foundation for wise choices, purpose, fulfillment, and inner peace and joy. These promises have the transformative ability to align your actions and mindset with His teachings. As you cultivate trust in His promises, they become a source of strength, hope, and guidance, leading to a deeper relationship with Him. As a reminder, Riley, God's Word contains countless promises you can explore in the "31-Day" framework. This framework delves into the significance and relevance of His promises in all aspects of life. With one promise for each day of the month, you can embrace His steadfast guarantees and welcome His blessings. No matter how late it may seem, you can find faith and fulfillment within just one month!

If you think of someone with horrible life decisions, do you ever say, "There is no hope for them"? Have you ever given up on someone because their past mistakes continue to influence their present choices? If so, a story from the Book of Luke will challenge your view on grace because God sees you differently. You'll discover that Jesus is always possible for everyone, no matter who you are or what you've done.

Later, Jesus encountered a man who lived a life filled with poor choices and wrongdoing. He was known to be a wicked, terrible sinner who took advantage of others. However, in his final moments, he decided to put his faith in Jesus. It is an impactful tale that showcases God's unwavering emphasis on forgiveness. The scene takes place at The Cross, where authorities falsely accused Jesus and subjected him to brutal beatings before making him carry His cross to the site of his execution. Crucifixion was a ruthless and gruesome method of death used by the Roman Empire to prolong the suffering of those condemned. As the soldiers hammered nails into Jesus' body, each breath inflicted excruciating pain upon him. He remained hanging on that cross, crucified as atonement for our sins.

As authorities were about to crucify Jesus, a criminal hung on either side of him, both punished for their crimes. One revolutionary taunted Jesus, challenging him to save them all. But Jesus remained silent in the face of the insults. The other criminal then speaks out, revealing a powerful message of God's love and mercy. He scolds the first criminal, reminding him they face the same punishment for their actions. This man openly accepts responsibility for his sins and acknowledges that he deserves to die for them. In a few moments, as he approaches death, he embarks on a journey toward eternal life through his newfound relationship with Jesus.

During the initial hours on the cross, the two nearby revolutionaries approached their deaths in alignment with their usual behavior. The situation filled them with cursing and bitterness. However, as time passed, one of the men observed Jesus' response to his suffering and recognized that he was unlike any other. He stopped cursing and took responsibility for his actions in a last-minute change of heart. He didn't blame society, his upbringing, or his companions. Instead, he acknowledged his wrongdoing by stating, "We are receiving what we deserve for our actions." This act of confessing guilt is crucial in establishing a relationship with Jesus. It entails owning up to one's sins, errors, and disappointments rather than making excuses. So, take ownership of your circumstances and mistakes instead of deflecting responsibility. Imagine if I were to ask you to participate in a demonstration for this lesson's sake; all you have to do is hold this sign. I will compensate you $10 at the end of this chapter, Sherry.

Most importantly, salvation begins with honesty towards God. Admitting that we cannot handle our problems and have sinned against Him and others is crucial. We can make progress when we take responsibility for our actions. Acknowledging our sins and being truthful about our current state allows us to see the gap between us and God, which seems impossible. Sometimes, it may feel like He is too far away, and we will never bridge the distance. However, taking ownership of our wrongdoing is necessary to close that gap. It can be challenging to admit when we are wrong, but as Romans 3:23 says, "All have sinned and fallen short of the glory of God." Even if we think we are good people or have done good deeds like donating money or attending church regularly, the truth remains that we have all sinned. Some individuals may have attended church for years without confessing their guilt to God. In 1 John 1:8, the Bible reminds us that claiming to be without sin is self-deception. Instead, if we confess our sins, God is faithful and will forgive us and purify us from all unrighteousness.

By claiming to have not sinned, you make God out to be a liar, and His word has no place in your life. Confession is necessary for forgiveness, and this applies to Christians as well. Taking responsibility for mistakes and failures is vital in our Christian walk. As the thief on the cross acknowledged, "They're punishing us justly; we are getting what our deeds deserve" (Lk. 23:41). However, he also recognized Jesus' innocence and turned his attention towards Him with dignity and majesty. In doing so, he took step two: confessing Jesus' innocence. So Dorothy, thank you for your assistance in recalling this step. I promise to be generous as we continue on this journey together. Please hold this sign to remind us of the importance of confession. Thank you again!

In recent years, the church has been under scrutiny for various issues. We have faced criticism for being angry, judgmental, out of touch, and not doing enough to help others. Additionally, folks have accused the church of being too involved in politics, being hypocritical, and even ulterior motives when it comes to people's money. Unfortunately, some of these criticisms hold truth. However, solely focusing on these negative aspects can create a distorted view. It is crucial also to acknowledge the positive aspects of the church.

Similarly, fixating on what is wrong can cause us to overlook the good things and blessings in other aspects of our lives. For instance, if we only see the flaws in our marriage or job, we may disregard all the valuable qualities that make them worth fighting for. Focusing solely on faults in school or with our children can lead us to miss opportunities and positive experiences. Even in our lives, if we only dwell on one problem or mistake, we may overlook all the blessings surrounding us. The same applies to the church – if we only see its flaws, we may miss out on recognizing its many virtues and purposes.

What sets the church apart is its unwavering connection to Jesus. While there may be flaws in churchgoers, leaders, and denominational systems, Jesus remains faultless and steadfast. His actions align with his words, and we can always rely on Him to be faithful and unwavering. This fact is the beauty of it all – Jesus' perfection makes up for our imperfections. As an imperfect community, we can never achieve perfection, but we can strive to be a healthy church that guides one another toward the perfect example of Jesus. Our focus is not on human personalities, programs, or ministry methods but on Jesus at the core of our existence. If the church disillusions you, perhaps you're focusing on the wrong aspect – shift your eyes from people to Jesus.

Therefore, the thief was right when he followed his confession of guilt with an open declaration of Jesus' innocence, "This man has done nothing wrong." Now, how do you confess Jesus' innocence?

What does it mean? It's the recognition that God planned for authorities to crucify Jesus so that God could forgive our sins. In his final moments, a thief acknowledged Jesus as the Son of God, the

Messiah, and the Savior of the world. He understood he could ask Jesus to remember him when entering His kingdom. Despite not knowing how to pray or what words to use, the thief took the third step: declaring his faith in Jesus by saying, "Remember me when You come into Your kingdom." So, Jessie, can you assist me with this display? You've heard about it. Please wear this sign as a show of support for us as we return to step three. I pledge to be charitable.

"DECLARE MY FAITH IN JESUS"

The thief on the cross declared, "Remember me when you come into Your kingdom." In this statement, we can see three elements of faith. Despite being tortured and crucified, he held onto his belief that the spirit does not die with the body. He recognized that there was something beyond this life, and in his final moments, he asked Jesus to remember him in His kingdom. Many people do not share this belief; they see death as an abrupt end without any hope for an afterlife. This man's faith extended beyond death, and it was a significant realization that there is indeed life after this one. When we pass from this earth, we will go to either heaven or hell – a thought worth reflecting on.

Secondly, he believed Jesus had a kingdom. To have faith in Him at the moment was to have unbelievable faith. Think about it: authorities had stripped Him of everything. His followers were gone.

They ruined His reputation. They even used His clothes as a prize in a gambling game. He seemingly hadn't a thing. There was a title over His' head which read, "King of the Jews." And we look at that today and say, "Well, that's a proper title." But that's not the way Pilot meant it. He was speaking to the Jews, "If you guys ever get a king, this is what'll happen to him. He'll be a condemned criminal on a cross and powerless to resist Roman rule." Pilot meant the title as an insult and joke. The thief looked at Jesus, who seemingly hadn't a thing, and said, "You got a kingdom." There was a tremendous amount of faith in that statement.

Additionally, the thief recognized the ongoing existence of the spirit after death and acknowledged Jesus's authority as a King. He believed that Jesus could show him mercy and help despite not having the opportunity to reconcile his past actions, grow spiritually, be baptized, or take communion. Similarly, Jesus saved and remembered him. The thief on the cross was the first to accept Jesus's sacrifice on the cross as atonement for his sins. And like us, we can also pray, "Jesus, I admit that I have sinned (which the Bible defines). I understand that you did not deserve to die, but you willingly took my place on the cross. I confess your death on the cross as payment for my transgressions. Please forgive me and be Lord over my life. I desire to live for you now and in eternity." The thief humbly pleaded, "Please remember me when you establish your kingdom."

In light of this, how does one respond to suffering? When in pain, the focus tends to be on self rather than others. During a splitting headache or the flu, it may not be the most appropriate time to ask for a favor. Instead, it is more fitting to inquire about the well-being of the person in distress. However, in a unique situation, even a desperate thief appealed to Jesus as he faced death. Instead of asking for money, he asked Jesus to remember him. And in turn, Jesus showed great compassion and promised him a place in paradise. Despite weighing his sins and their impact on eternity, Jesus accepted and forgave him based on his confession of guilt, declaration of faith in Jesus's innocence, and plea for mercy. Howard, could you lend me a hand? I truly appreciate your kindness and would like you to wear this small token as a reminder of my gratitude towards you.

Indeed, Jesus willingly welcomed the thief. Until this point, you have logically adhered to the plan. Correct? However, this is where you face difficulty. How can Jesus extend forgiveness to the thief? How can Jesus promise him a place in heaven? After all, he is a criminal, having led a terrible life and undeserving of redemption. While the disciples faithfully followed Jesus and endured persecution, this man selfishly stole from others. While the disciples suffered and made sacrifices, he continued with his wrongdoings. And now, at the end of his life, he suddenly chooses to follow Jesus. Who does he think he is? How dare he wait until now to plan for Jesus?

Hence, we require assistance regarding this matter. We have doubts about death-row conversions and death-bed confessions. It's difficult to understand why God would forgive individuals who have led terrible lives and only make a life-changing decision at the very end. Is it fair that someone who accepts Jesus right before their death receives the same reward in heaven as someone who has devoted their entire life to him? In essence, can you connect this choice to my demonstration? Much gratitude to Sherry, Dorothy, Jessie, and Howard for displaying the signs. I highly appreciate your contribution in conveying this message. Howard, as promised, here's ten dollars for your invaluable help. Jessie, thank you so much! Your support drove home the point, and here's another 10 dollars as a token of appreciation. How are you both holding up, Sherry and Dorothy? Are you doing well? Excellent! Dorothy, here's ten bucks as a token of my appreciation for your contribution. And Michael, as I had promised earlier, here's ten dollars for your assistance. Thank you once again for all your support!

Similarly, you may currently be facing challenges and questioning the fairness of the situation. You might think, "Hold on, this doesn't seem right. How can Howard receive the same payment as everyone else when he only joined in a few minutes ago? Is that fair? He received the same reward for a short time, while the others put in longer hours. And what about Sherry? She dedicated more time than anyone else but received the same amount. Doesn't that feel unjust? Jesus recognized that we would struggle with this concept, so He shared a parable with His disciples (Mt. 20:1-16): In this story, Jesus compared God's kingdom to an estate manager who went out early in the morning to hire workers for his vineyard. They agreed on a daily wage and began their work. Throughout the day, the manager hired more workers from around town at nine, noon, and three o'clock. He found even more idle men at five o'clock and gave them work. When evening came, and it was time for payment, the owner instructed his foreman to start with the last hired and work back to the first.

Logically, the workers who only put in a few hours would differ from those who worked all day. Despite this, they all received the same payment of one dollar. Upon receiving their pay, they complained to the manager, expressing frustration that their co-workers who only worked for an hour were considered equal to them, who toiled all day in the scorching heat. The manager responded to the spokesperson, stating that he was not being unfair as they had all agreed upon a wage of one dollar. He reminded them that it was his prerogative to distribute his money as he saw fit and, therefore, instructed them to take their pay and leave. He explained that he decided to give the same amount to the worker who arrived last as he had done for those who had been there longer.

To reiterate, Jesus used the analogy of an estate manager to illustrate that latecomers who accept Him with their dying breath will receive the same forgiveness as those who've served Him their entire lives. Your response may be similar to the workers who labored all day and questioned the fairness of this. However, God is abundant in His forgiveness and love, extending it to all regardless of their stage in life. The principle remains: Jesus is always available, making it possible to follow Him anytime. Therefore, waiting until the last minute may seem like a sound plan if we knew when our last minute would be, but unfortunately, we do not have that assurance. We cannot predict what tomorrow holds, and there are no guarantees.

On the other hand, there is also a danger of waiting too long or thinking we need to fix ourselves before coming to God. This mindset does not make sense because if we could improve ourselves independently, we would have already done so. Instead of waiting any longer, why not come to Jesus now?

The thief sought more time to improve himself, whether it was tackling his bad habits, addictions, or behaviors. He approached God in his current state and received absolution—no need to tidy up or discard vices before embracing Jesus. Salvation does not require new clothes, tossing out cigarettes, or altering behaviors - that's not the way it works. Instead, come to Jesus with all your flaws and failures, including sins, habits, and addictions. Come as you are and confess your transgressions, seeking forgiveness. God intends not to change you; He desires to forgive and establish a relationship with you. Through this connection and incorporating His teachings into your life, transformation naturally responds to His love. So, you may be curious about how this applies to you.

God's amazing grace is available to all. Every soul holds significance to Him, and His love knows no boundaries. If you believe, there is no doubt that God's love also extends to you. Your past or present should not hold you back from accepting Jesus into your life - in fact, it makes you the perfect candidate for His forgiveness. And not only does He forgive, but He also forgets your sins. Riley, I want to offer my support and encouragement as you embark on this journey with Jesus. Is there anything specific that you need guidance on? Remember, Jesus will always be by your side. Are you ready to confess your sins to Him and acknowledge His innocence? Will you open your heart and receive His forgiveness, grace, and mercy? Are you prepared to follow Him wholeheartedly and receive the promise of eternal life? That person is YOU! I will pray for you, and I know that just like the thief on the cross, you can take the same steps towards redemption - confessing your sins and acknowledging Jesus as your Lord. Believe in Him, turn away from sinfulness, live for Him, and follow His teachings. If you abide in His Word and remain faithful to Him, whatever you ask for, He'll grant it.

Lord, we humbly ask for your help and forgiveness. We acknowledge our mistake in categorizing people and questioning their eligibility for your grace and forgiveness. Please forgive us for judging others based on their actions or appearances, especially those we see on the news or those who have committed terrible acts. We realize now that no one is too far gone for you to love them and offer them your grace and forgiveness. We are truly sorry, Lord. Instead, please guide us to see people through your eyes – as your beloved children and creations – so we may extend your love, grace, and mercy to even the "worst of the worst." Remind us always that you have a plan full of hope for everyone.

# APPENDIX

## *Self-Declare: Encouraging Bible Truths About God's Promises*

---

### 2Pe. 3:9

The Lord is not slow in keeping his promise, as some understand slowness. Instead, he is patient with you, not wanting anyone to perish, but everyone to come to repentance.

### 2Co. 7:1

Therefore, since we have these promises, dear friends, let us purify ourselves from everything that contaminates body and spirit, perfecting holiness out of reverence for God.

### 2Co. 1:20

For no matter how many promises God has made, they are "Yes" in Christ. And so, through him the "Amen" is spoken by us to the glory of God.

### He. 10:23

Let us hold unswervingly to the hope we profess, for he who promised is faithful.

### Ph. 4:19

And my God will meet all your needs according to the riches of his glory in Christ Jesus.

1Jn. 1:9

If we confess our sins, he is faithful and just and will forgive us our sins and purify us from all unrighteousness.

Ro. 6:23

For the wages of sin is death, but the gift of God is eternal life in[a] Christ Jesus our Lord.

He. 6:13

When God made his promise to Abraham, since there was no one greater for him to swear by, he swore by himself,

Nu. 30:2

When a man makes a vow to the LORD or takes an oath to obligate himself by a pledge, he must not break his word but must do everything he said.

2Co. 5:17

Therefore, if anyone is in Christ, the new creation has come:[a] The old has gone, the new is here!

2Pe. 1:3-4

His divine power has given us everything we need for a godly life through our knowledge of him who called us by his own glory and goodness. Through these he has given us his very great and precious promises, so that through them you may participate in the divine nature, having escaped the corruption in the world caused by evil desires.

Je. 29:11-13

For I know the plans I have for you," declares the LORD, "PLANS TO PROSPER YOU AND NOT TO HARM YOU, PLANS TO GIVE YOU HOPE AND A FUTURE. Then you will call on me and come and pray to me, and I will listen to you. You will seek me and find me when you seek me with all your heart.

Dt. 31:6

Be strong and courageous. Do not be afraid or terrified because of them, for the LORD your God goes with you; he will never leave you nor forsake you.

Is. 41:10

So do not fear, for I am with you; do not be dismayed, for I am your God. I will strengthen you and help you; I will uphold you with my righteous right hand.

2Ti. 3:16

All Scripture is God-breathed and is useful for teaching, rebuking, correcting, and training in righteousness,

Mt. 11:28-29

"Come to me, all you who are weary and burdened, and I will give you rest. Take my yoke upon you and learn from me, for I am gentle and humble in heart, and you will find rest for your souls.

Ps. 84:11

For the LORD GOD IS A SUN AND SHIELD; THE LORD BESTOWS FAVOR AND HONOR; NO GOOD THING DOES HE WITHHOLD FROM THOSE WHOSE WALK IS BLAMELESS.

Ja. 1:5

If any of you lacks wisdom, you should ask God, who gives generously to all without finding fault, and it will be given to you.

Je. 30:17

But I will restore you to health and heal your wounds,' declares the LORD, 'BECAUSE YOU ARE CALLED AN OUTCAST, ZION FOR WHOM NO ONE CARES.

Jn. 16:13

But when he, the Spirit of truth, comes, he will guide you into all the truth. He will not speak on his own; he will speak only what he hears, and he will tell you what is yet to come.

# *ACKNOWLEDGMENTS*

Dear Friend, As you reach the end of this book, you have my deepest gratitude for the time you've spent delving into these pages.

Many people helped me prepare this text. I give honor to whom honor is due. First and foremost, I thank almighty God! He enabled me with faithfulness, gifts, and favor. May all I put my hands to bring glory to His Kingdom, equip disciples to do His work, and build up the church.

I'm grateful for family and friends who prayed and supported me in writing this book. I penned this book not with pen and ink but with the Spirit of the living God. I pray I've carved these words in your heart. And they're good, helpful, and encouraging. I hope these multiplied blessings touch your soul and affect those who have eyes but refuse to see and ears but refuse to hear.

Lord God Almighty, make your face shine upon me so I reach the most significant number of new and growing believers likely to draw nearer to you!

# *REVIEW ASK*

If you enjoyed this book, please leave a review! Your feedback will help us improve future releases.

I'd also appreciate your honest reviews on Amazon, Goodreads, BookBub, and markcoverton.com.

Let's share God's Word by writing a review about the Assignment! I read all reviews and use your feedback to make future books even better for you.

Amazon.com/author/markoverton

http://www.goodreads.com/author/7647613.Mark_C_Overton

BookBub.com/profile/mark-c-overton

Ask an Authorgraph at https://www.authorgraph.com/authors/goodnewsbookset.

Your reviews matter a lot to us, and we thank you endlessly! On the other hand, the most essential write-up is you yourselves. Your life is a letter written in my heart; everyone can read it and recognize the good work among you. Indeed, you are a letter from Christ showing the result of ministry among you.

# READ OTHER BOOKS BY MARK C. OVERTON

"True Words for True Believers"

Win at Work

*Church Leader Series*

Assignment

Crossroads


Second Editions

Faith Transformation, 2nd Edition

LORD, Teach Me How to Pray, 2nd Edition.

*Faith Series*

Faith Excellence

Faith Transformation


*The Good Book Series*

New Day, New Life (Series Compilation)

What Love Really Means

You Only Live Once

I Like to Start with Something Funny

LORD, Teach Me How to Pray

Chapter and Verse

Airmen Series

Career Progression Guide for Airmen: The Basics

Career Progression Guide for Airmen

Faith Builder | Faith Influencer | For Lifelong Faith Followers

## DISCOVER BONUS BOOK CONTENT

I can only offer so much in this book, but you can watch trailers for each book at https://youtube.com/@truewordsalways.

The world of social media has exploded in recent years because of story. The power of story can connect and motivate people, to be further involved in each other lives, and to care for and have compassion for others.

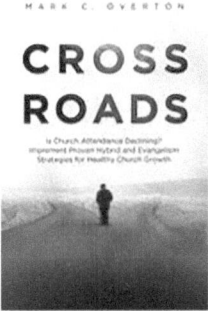

www.ingramcontent.com/pod-product-compliance
Lightning Source LLC
Chambersburg PA
CBHW031440120626
46545CB00006B/2499